THE POTTERY
HAND BOOK

THE POTTERY
HANDBOOK

JOSIE WARSHAW

Published by SILVERDALE BOOKS
An imprint of Bookmart Ltd
Registered number 2372865
Trading as Bookmart Ltd
Blaby Road
Wigston
Leicester LE18 4SE

© 2005 D&S Books Ltd

D&S Books Ltd
Kerswell
Parkham Ash, Bideford
Devon, England
EX39 5PR

e-mail us at:
enquiries@d-sbooks.co.uk

This edition printed 2005

ISBN 1-856058-72-7

DS0108. Pottery Handbook

Creative director: Sarah King
Editor: Nicky Barber
Project editor: Clare Haworth-Maden
Designer: 2H Design
Photographer: Stephen Brayne

Set in Adobe Garamond, with headings in Trajan

Printed in China

1 3 5 7 9 10 8 6 4 2

CONTENTS

INTRODUCTION

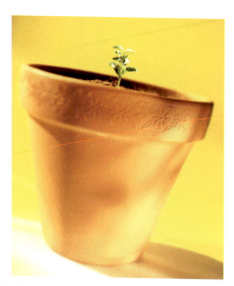

Clay surrounds us.

Clay is all around us. Its properties and uses are so varied that it is often taken for granted. Unwittingly, it is used every day by almost everyone, in items ranging from eating utensils to computer chips. When used for personal creative purposes, its versatility and various appearances begin to be understood and appreciated.

Anyone working with clay can use its great range of properties for self-expression, directing material, processes and techniques into an expression of their own personality. This creative expression is open to all and is not the reserve of the fine artist or craftsperson. This book is written as an aid to the learning of the processes and techniques required to make your own imaginings in clay. It will help to build up your knowledge of making and decorating with this wonderfully versatile, tactile material.

The projects in the book aim to cover a range of hand-building and throwing techniques. The projects are designed as a guide to show how to approach different types of forms – straight-sided, curved, solid and hollowed – when hand-building, and how to make open or closed forms when throwing. There is also guidance from the start of the creative process, when selecting a clay, through to how to fire your own finished work.

DESIGN

Clay is the most versatile of materials. Any desired colour or effect can be applied to its surface, but before choosing this outer veneer, there is the question of what form the work will take. What is the initial idea or motivation? Will the work be functional or sculptural?

Design using clay emerges through a progression of experiments with ideas, forms and materials. Materials and techniques go back through history, so that anyone exploring clay-work today uses similar concepts and methods to those used by past artists and craftspeople. Knowledge of materials and techniques was emulated and shared, exchanged as a result of travel, trade, commercial competition, scientific endeavour, collecting and pure admiration. Contemporary ceramics represent a cross-fertilization of time-honoured traditions and aesthetics, which stem from cultures and civilisations around the world and through history.

The freedom, when designing, to make sculptural or decorative work is tempered by the constraints of the materials and the firing process. A functional or sculptural form is designed as an entity with its applied surface to give an individual characteristic to the work. The way in which the surface is applied is a personal choice that comes from within each maker. Like all design practice, the choices made are governed by observation and thought. Knowledge of design can be learnt not just in museums and galleries, but also by closely observing everyday things, such as textiles, natural objects or buildings.

The reasoning behind a design, the individuality of the maker and the way in which a piece of work is made are all considerations that have an influence on the finished work. Practical solutions, striving for innovation or perfection in form and surface design, are challenges that grip and occupy the minds of all clay-workers at whatever level they are working. Knowledge of clay comes about through experimentation and exploration, which is otherwise known as hands-on experience!

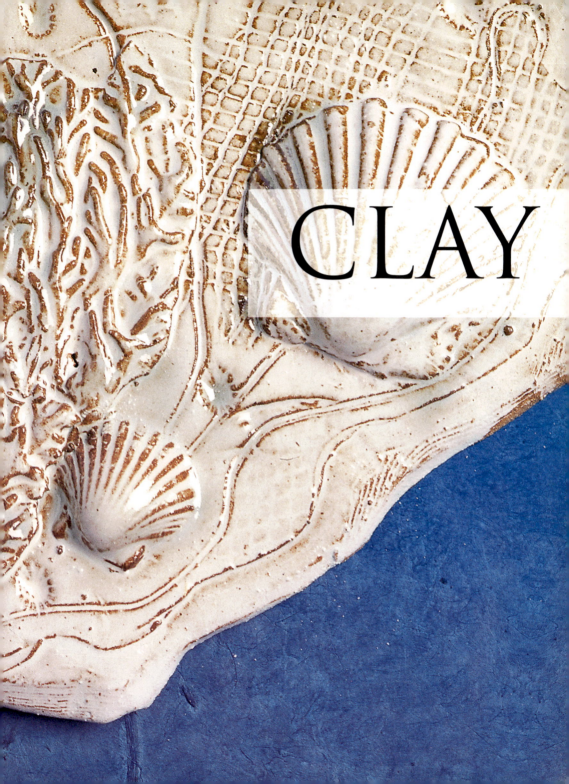

CLAY

WHAT IS CLAY?

The Earth's surface was formed from melted rock that cooled and solidified. Over millions of years, the weathering action of freezing and thawing, the grinding of glaciers and the beating of rain, rivers and streams, slowly broke the Earth's crust into boulders, then stones, then pebbles and finally into small particles. Feldspathic or granite rock, which is the most abundant mineral on the Earth's surface, was transformed over time by this decomposition and weathering and is the basis of clay. Clays from different locations are made up of differing amounts of oxides formed by oxygen combining with minerals. The varying proportions of clay constituents give each clay its own, individual qualities.

China clay, or kaolin, is very pure and is used as an ingredient to give strength and whiteness to porcelain. Ball clays, often blue or black in their unfired state, give plasticity to a clay. They lose their organic colouring when fired to become white or buff. Red clays contain iron oxide, which acts as a flux, commonly fired at low temperatures. Commercially bought clays are a controlled mix of different clays.

Other materials used in clay bodies include grog, which is ground high-fired clay, molochite and sand. These materials are used as openers to reduce the shrinkage rate of a clay and therefore its drying and firing stress. Openers can be added to any clay to make it suitable for such items as tiles, so that they do not overly shrink and warp when drying (see page 20, kneading in additions). Grog often has the added quality of bleeding through certain glazes that are fired at high temperatures to give an interesting speckled effect.

Obtaining and selecting your clay

Clay can be bought ready-prepared from a ceramic supplier in a plastic state. It is packaged in sealed, 25kg or 12.5kg polythene bags. The larger the amount of clay ordered, the cheaper it becomes per kilogram, and the more cost-efficient it is to have it delivered. (The carriage charge can be as much for the delivery of 6 bags as that of 40 bags.)

Each clay has a certain handling quality, colour, temperature range and plasticity (or workability). These qualities are indicated in suppliers' catalogues, but can be assessed much better by feel. The choice is wide, and can be made even wider by combining clays. Clays can be intermixed at the plastic stage (see page 17, preparing clay), one body with another, to bring them to a required workability or openness, while at the same time altering the colour and texture if so desired.

Ceramic-supply catalogues also supply information about temperature ranges for clays, suitability for different techniques, textures, fired colours and, of course, prices. Most clays are suitable for all techniques, but there are many that are specifically designed for a particular forming method, for example, a white clay body developed for throwing purposes, or a crank that is open and so particularly strong for hand-building large, sculptural pieces. The range also depends on which ceramic supplier you are using. Selecting a clay is done at the designing stage, and is influenced by the choices of format, scale, the finished surface and, above all, the overall 'feel' of the work that is being visualised.

The clay temperature range

Clays can be subdivided into the following three main temperature ranges.

**Earthenware has a maturing range
of 1,000–1,180°C**

Earthenware is porous and light. When fired, it is easily chipped. Terracotta plant pots, bricks and commercially-made tableware fall into this category as they are all fired at a low temperature. If it is unglazed, liquids can seep through earthenware. The sound made by earthenware when it is tapped is a low 'clunk'.

**Stoneware has a maturing range
of 1,200–1,300°C**

Stoneware is made at a higher temperature range than earthenware and is therefore better at holding liquids and is not so easily broken. It is called stoneware as it is dense like stone, and it rings higher when it is tapped.

**Porcelain has a maturing range
of 1,280–1,350°C**

When fired at these high temperatures, porcelain becomes translucent because its particles are dense and vitreous like glass. Porcelain makes a very high 'ping' sound when tapped.

(Coloured clays, such as those used for making the beads in the bead project (see page 99), have different temperature ranges for firing, from 1,040°C to 1,220°C, depending on what type of clay is used. The colouring oxides used to stain the clays act as a flux and bring the temperature range down. Check with the supplier's catalogue or make tests before you fire coloured clays.)

When listed in a catalogue, a clay will often be referred to as 'maturing' or vitrifying at a certain temperature. This is the point at which a body reaches its optimum strength and compactness. Below this temperature, the body is underfired, and will underachieve its strength and density. Conversely, if a clay body is fired beyond its maturing temperature, such faults as warping, bloating and collapsing can occur. At the far end of this scale, the clay will be transformed into a completely molten state. In the case of porcelain, a state of near-complete fusion is obtained, resulting in its translucent qualities when the wall is thin.

Armed with this information, it is necessary to select a clay that is not only suitable for the kind of work in mind, but also to select a temperature range suitable for the glaze that is going to be applied and the type of firing that the glaze will be subjected to (see opposite, the clay temperature range; see also page 248, glaze-firing).

Clay shrinkage and plasticity

As clay dries and fires, it shrinks at an approximate rate of 10 per cent, the highest shrinkage rate taking place from plastic to the bone-dry state. A clay with a higher shrinkage rate than this is very difficult to work, but such clays can be 'opened up' by kneading materials into them. Grog is fired clay that has been ground up and can be bought in a variety of graded particle sizes, ranging from dust to grit. Either grog or sand can be worked into clay in this way to improve its workability.

The more open a clay, the less plastic it will become, so care must be taken not to make too many additions to your clay. Clays that are very dense and plastic, and therefore have a high shrinkage rate, can pose problems because they move and warp more when drying and firing. When slab-building or joining handles, a high shrinkage rate also increases the chances of cracks forming at joining points during drying and firing. Surfaces that need to be flat can warp or curl at the edges when dried and/or fired. Drying your work slowly by wrapping it in polythene and firing it slowly can get around some of these problems, but if it does not, then open up the clay that you are using.

Grog or sand can be kneaded into plastic clay to reduce its shrinkage rate. These additions can be done by weight or visually, by volume. To test how much grog you can add to a clay without losing plasticity, a simple plasticity test can be made by rolling a coil of clay about 2cm wide and bending it over while still in its plastic state to form a ring. If the clay cracks when forming the ring, the clay is known to be 'short' and difficult to work. If this is the case, then the amount of opener that you add to that clay should be reduced.

You can test a clay body to find out how much it shrinks by rolling out a sheet of plastic clay approximately 1 to 2cm thick and cutting it into strips about 14cm long and 4cm wide. While the clay is still plastic, accurately score 10cm-long lines with a knife tip onto the clay strips. Now allow the marked strips to dry slowly on a flat surface, turning them frequently. Note the lengths of the scored lines when the strips have become bone dry, and again after they have been fired to their intended temperature. You can then assess the dry and the fired shrinkage rate of your clay. If the final shrinkage rate from plastic to fired exceeds 10 to 13 per cent, your clay will be difficult to use and additions should be made to alter it.

Consistency

Your clay should be soft enough to move, but firm enough that it does not stick to hands and surfaces. If it is a struggle in either direction, more clay – either softer or firmer, depending on which way the clay needs to go – can be wedged into the mass. It will not take long to acquire a feel for the correct 'give' or consistency for the particular job in hand.

The consistency of your clay will affect your ability to use the material. For example, firmer clay will allow you a longer working time when throwing a curved, thin-walled shape on the wheel. On the other hand, softer clay used for a coil will allow you to attach it with less pressure being applied to the supporting form to which it is to be attached and so prevent the supporting form from buckling as you smear it into position.

Clay that is too wet can be wedged on dry plaster slabs (see page 22, reclaiming or reconstituting clay, and page 24, making a plaster bat) until enough moisture has been extracted to give a usable,

plastic state. If the clay is too firm and no soft clay is available to change the mass, the clay can only be left to become dry for reclamation. Clay that is 'on the turn' of becoming too firm can be saved by making holes in the mass, pouring water in and then wedging it in, or alternatively, and less strenuously, by soaking the clay in a bag or container with water and leaving it to soften.

These are the tools that you will need for preparing your clay:
wire (1);
a plaster bat (2);
polythene (3);
a pair of scales and a set of weights (4); and
a paint-scraper (5).

CLAY STORAGE, PREPARATION AND RECLAIMING

Clay can be stored for many years in the airtight, polythene bags in which it is purchased, provided that the seal is not opened or the bag is not punctured. If a bag does get torn, it can be sealed with strong, plastic, sticky tape to prevent air from reaching the clay. Clay can also be stored in an airtight container, such as a plastic bucket with a sealed lid.

For shorter periods, clay can be wrapped in sheets of polythene to prevent it from drying, a system that is also used to retain any clay-work at the leather-hard stage.

Preparation

Whether it be hand-built or wheel-thrown, it is important that your clay is first made workable by coaxing it into a homogenous state. To prepare your clay, you need to wedge and knead it to ensure that it is of a uniform consistency throughout its mass. The same technique is used when intermixing clays.

You will need a suitable area or worktop that is solidly fixed into position. A concrete paving stone makes an ideal heavy clay-preparation surface. Your preparation surface should be at a comfortable height, roughly at the top of the thighs. If surplus clay becomes caked on the surface of your preparation area, you can scrape it away with a flat-headed paint-scraper.

Wedging and kneading clay

WEDGING CLAY

1. Cut your mass of clay into smaller pieces using a cutting wire.

2. Reassemble the pieces by slamming them back down in a different order on top of one another. Lift up each piece to shoulder height and slam it down onto the piece below, reassembling and turning the faces into a new order as you work.

Do not try to wedge too much clay together at once.

KNEADING CLAY

Kneading is a rhythmic, physical exercise that should not be overly strenuous.

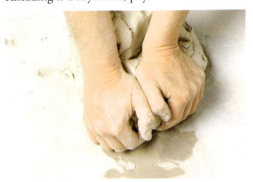

1. To make the work of kneading more comfortable, stand with your feet far apart, one foot slightly in front of the other. Move your body forwards when you apply weight to the mass with the heel of your hand.

2. Then lean back and repeat the rhythmic motion of rocking forwards and backwards while you apply pressure to the mass of clay, pushing down at the point of the forward roll.

3. Turn the clay with your left hand and rock your body, using the heel of your right hand and a straight right arm to apply downward pressure. Rock the clay back and then forwards, turning the mass a hand-width and reapplying downward pressure until you have completed an entire rotation of the mass that you are preparing.

4. Cut the clay and check it for lumps, air pockets and foreign bodies. Continue to knead it until the mass is even.

KNEADING IN ADDITIONS

1. Sand or grog can be added to the plastic clay at additions of approximately 10 to 20 per cent, depending on the clay and what is being added. Note that it is easier to knead additions into clay that is of a soft consistency.

2. The additions are kneaded into the clay to reduce its shrinkage rate (see page 14, clay shrinkage) or to provide texture or colour.

Preparing clay for throwing on the wheel

Scales are used to weigh prepared clay into equal-sized balls in preparation for throwing on the wheel.

These typical weights for the following shapes and sizes can be used as a rough guide.

Cylinder	13cm high	10cm wide	weight 5kg
Bowl	7.5cm high	15.5cm wide	weight 5kg
Four-cup teapot	11.5cm high	7cm wide	weight 7kg
Jug	18cm high	10cm wide	weight 7kg
Turned plate	3.5cm high	30cm wide	weight 1.6kg

To make a run of work that you require to be of the same size, weigh and shape the clay into balls ready to put onto the wheelhead. You can use the weight suggestions shown above as a rough guide.

If you are learning to throw, take a dozen or so pieces to the wheel to allow for uninterrupted practice. When trying out a new shape on the wheel, keep a note of the weight of clay that you used to make a particular size. This will be useful information if you later want to repeat that same shape on the wheel.

When you have finished preparing and weighing your clay balls to throw on the wheel, put them in a plastic bowl and cover the top with polythene to prevent air from drying them out on the surface before you use them. Note that if they come into contact with a porous surface, they will become firm on one side before you have used them, making them difficult to centre and throw.

Reclaiming or reconstituting clay

If your clay has become too dry to work with, it can be reclaimed to be used again by soaking it down and spreading it out on a thick, smooth plaster slab. Clay that is too wet or sticky to use can also be brought to the required consistency by being kneaded on a dry plaster slab. However, once your clay has been fired in the kiln, it cannot be reclaimed because it has been transformed by the heat of the firing.

1. To prepare your clay for reconstitution, you must first leave it to become bone dry by breaking or cutting it into small pieces, thus allowing greater contact with the air, and then leaving it. You will see when it has become bone dry as it will then appear lighter in colour.

2. When the clay is completely dry, cover it with water (this is called 'slaking') and allow it to soak overnight, or until the clay's consistency resembles a thick slop.

3. Remove the excess water that has settled on the top by pouring or scooping it off.

4. Then spread a thick layer of clay onto your plaster bat. By turning the clay, you can bring more surface area into contact with the plaster, which will absorb moisture from the clay.

When the clay has reached a manageable state for kneading, it can be removed from the plaster bat. The length of time needed to reclaim clay will depend on the dryness of the plaster, the room temperature and the amount of clay being reclaimed. A covering sheet of polythene is sufficient to prevent your clay from drying out too much while being left unattended overnight.

Making a plaster bat for reclaiming clay

On a smooth board, such as plastic-coated chipboard, set up four board walls with internal measurements matching the size of your required plaster bat.

You will need: a surform blade (1); parcel tape (2); board walls (3); and a plastic bucket (4).

1. Support the walls well with string or parcel tape passed around their girth.

2. Seal and support the outside bottom edges of the walls with a good, thick coil of soft clay and smear it downwards to make a seal.

3. Seal the inside-corner seams with soft clay if there are any small gaps.

4. Estimate the amount of plaster that you will need to make your bat. Going on this estimation, measure about half of this amount as water, which you should pour into a plastic bucket. Gradually strew the plaster into the water until a small peak appears without dispersing on the surface of the water.

5. Mix the plaster thoroughly with your hand until it begins to feel heavier. This is the signal that the plaster is ready to be poured.

6. Quickly pour the plaster inside the four walls. (If you have any plaster left over, transfer it to a bin and do not pour it down the sink. Clean out the plaster residue in the bucket before it becomes hard.) Wait for 5 to 10 minutes for the plaster to become hot. You will now be able to remove the four walls, support clay and string or tape.

8. Take a surform blade and remove the sharp corners with it.

7. Remove the set plaster bat from the board.

9. To dry your plaster bat, prop it up somewhere warm so that air can circulate around it. It needs to be bone dry before you can use it to reclaim any clay.

JOINING

No matter how small the pieces are, clay must be joined using the following technique to create an effective bond. By being thorough with your joining, your work will not come apart during the drying and firing processes. First, you need to make slurry (clay glue).

To make slurry

Your slurry must match the clay that you are using. Tear up some clay into small pieces and allow them to become bone dry. (If the clay is not dry, it will not dissolve.) Completely cover the small, bone-dry pieces of clay with water. Allow the clay to dissolve before stirring the mixture to a consistency between single and double cream. Make an ample supply so that you do not have to keep repeating this process.

The technique

1. Apply slurry to the face of each piece to be joined using a stiff brush. Score and rough up the slurried faces with a knife tip. Doing this roughens the surface so that the joined clay will knit together to make a firm bond.

2. Push the two pieces together, giving them a slight wiggle as you do so, until the scored faces knit together.

3. Use a damp sponge, tool or paintbrush to remove any excess slurry emerging from the join.

Some tips for joining sheets or slabs of clay

When making a butted join, allow an extra length for an overlap that can be trimmed and cleaned up at the leather-hard stage.

When joining slabs to a base, stand the walls on the top of the base rather than at its sides. This will pull the walls in and prevent the work from coming apart at the seams.

Making a chamfered cut to a slab will allow it to sit at an angle. The degree of the chamfer will dictate the slant of the wall.

Let the work become leather-hard (firm) before giving the slurried seams a final trim and clean. This will give the work a cleaner finish.

To trim the base joins when a piece is leather-hard, drag it so that it hangs over the surface on which it is sitting for a clear line of attack for a hacksaw blade, kidney or other tool (see page 85, the lidded-box project).

Some tips for joining soft clay to soft clay

Soft, plastic clay can be overlapped to make a join by pushing or smearing the pieces together. If the clay has become somewhat firm, this method will not be effective, and slurry and scoring are required. Joining clay that has become too firm requires more pressure, which can distort the supporting form or cause it to weaken (see page 79, the soft-slab-dish project). You can join very soft slabs by pressing them together with a damp sponge or by pinching or pressing an overlap. The resulting seams can be left untouched to show the workings of the joining process.

Soft-slab joining on a former

Slabs can be wrapped around straight-sided formers, such as cardboard tubes. This is a fast method that is suitable for making cylinders or other shapes, such as ovals, before joining them to a base.

1. Tightly cover the former with a sheet of newspaper and secure it with sticky tape to keep it flat. Wrap the slab around the former, making an overlap, before cutting a chamfered edge by holding the knife at an angle as you run it along the overlapping slabs.

2. Remove the excess pieces before scoring and slurrying the angle-cut edges together.

3. Join the wrapped shape to its base while it is still on its former. The former must be removed before the shape is allowed to become firm and shrink onto it. The newspaper around the former will allow it to slide out of the shape without sticking to the soft clay. The excess at the base is then cut away, and further paring and cleaning of the shape is done once it has firmed to become leather-hard.

Some tips for joining soft clay to leather-hard clay

Soft, plastic clay can be joined to leather-hard clay only if it is slurried and scored into place.

Joining spouts and handles

To learn how to join such components as spouts and handles, see the teapot and jug projects, pages 142 to 144 and page 148.

Leather-hard – the workable state

Returning to a piece of clay-work once it has been allowed to become firm, or 'leather-hard', can produce favourable results. This cheese-like, leather-hard state can be recognised by the clay's cold feel and firmness.

At the leather-hard stage, clay is capable of supporting the weight of any further additions of applied clay without buckling or distorting. To make a strong bond between leather-hard clay and applied plastic or leather-hard clay, you need to use the slurry and score technique (see page 28). At this stage, the clay can meet the applied pressure needed for paring and smoothing with tools. It can also support the weight and stress required for such work as joining coils or handles, or turning out a foot-ring.

Once your clay moves beyond this leather-hard stage and starts to become dry, any joining will be unsuccessful. The dry state of clay is recognisable when the clay becomes lighter in colour. Be careful with work at this dry stage as the clay is very brittle and can break easily when knocked. Because it is dry, you will not be able to repair it by scoring and slurrying.

HAND-BUILDING

Hand-building is the term used to describe clay-work that does not rely on machinery. Methods of working for hand-building are less restricting than throwing on a wheel. When working on the wheel, there is always the imposition of a circular shape, but when hand-building, ideas can be expressed in any number of ways – and that's exciting!

This straight-sided box has been made using the leather-hard, slab-building technique.

This section introduces the main hand-building techniques: pinching, coiling, slab-building and modelling. Each technique is illustrated with a project idea. These techniques require very little equipment – just a table-top and a few tools. This section also covers press-moulding and illustrates how to make your own simple moulds.

You can follow each project through the book into the decorating, mould-making, glazing and firing sections. This will help to build your understanding of the different processes and decorative treatments involved in clay-work. If you are new to working with clay, the clay-preparation section (see page 17) explains what you need to do before you start working with the clay. The information in the joining section applies to all of the hand-building techniques. Each of the techniques explained can be used on its own or can be combined with other techniques to create your own finished work.

TOOLS

1 **Potter's knife:** a clay knife with a pointed tip so as not to drag on the clay.

2 **Metal/serrated kidney:** to pare and smooth walls.

3 **Hacksaw blade:** to pare and carve clay.

4 **Surform blade:** to level a rim, pare a thick wall and clean up a plaster mould.

5 **Wooden modelling tools:** to shape clay and to work into areas that are not reachable with the fingers.

6 **Hooped modelling tools:** to scoop clay out of solid forms.

7 **Sponge:** to smooth out tool marks.

8 **Harp wire:** to cut slabs or to trim edges.

9 **Rolling slats:** to keep slabs even in section when rolling them out.

10 **Rolling pin:** to roll out clay into sheets.

11 **Rubber kidney:** to finalise a press-moulded surface.

12 **Rolling cloth:** to roll out slabs without them sticking to a work surface.

13 **Hole-cutters:** to cut holes cleanly.

14 **Wooden boards:** to store, carry or stack work.

15 **Banding wheel:** to turn work.

16 **Polythene:** to retain work in the leather-hard condition.

17 **Paintbrush/plastic pot:** to apply slurry.

18 **Paint-stripper:** to speed up drying.

PINCHING TECHNIQUES

When pinching-out clay, there is the potential to create either a rhythmical, textured surface or a taut, flat surface by working over the pinched areas with tools at the leather-hard stage to smooth and even the wall. This is a useful method for creating a beginning to a piece of work, which can then be worked into any shape or form.

1. Using prepared, plastic clay (see page 17), take a ball that fits comfortably into your hand. Press your thumb down, into the centre of the ball, to within 5mm of where the base of the shape will be. Pinch out the bottom area of clay first, leaving the rim until last to avoid cracks forming. Starting at the deepest point of the ball, pinch the clay between your finger and thumb, rotating it as you do so.

2. Continue to rotate the ball as you pinch, starting at the base and progressing up to the top edge while supporting the opened ball in the palm of your other hand. Continue to turn and pinch with even pressure at finger-width intervals until the required thickness of wall is achieved. After some practice, you will be able to feel which points are the thickest and where greater pressure is needed to even out the wall.

3. Top edges and walls can be pinched to the thinness of paper. Alternatively, shapes can be left with a fat rim to make an adequate positioning surface for the addition of coils. (See also page 69, the pinched-bottle project, which shows how to join two pinched shapes together.)

Changing and manipulating the shape

Shapes can be eased out by stroking with the fingertips from the inside while supporting the shape in the other, non-working hand. Check the profile of the shape all the way round to ensure that the shape is consistent, or that it is the shape that you require.

If the shape turns outwards too far, it can be brought back in while it is still soft. To bring a shape inwards, gather or fold the wall and squeeze it together.

Alternatively, you could cut 'V' shapes out of the rim, or leaf-shaped cuts out of a bellied wall. Remove the cut shapes before pushing and smoothing the rim or belly back together again.

If cracks appear at the rim, smooth them down with a finger or smooth in a piece of very soft clay. They can also be removed by cutting them away with the tip of a pointed potter's knife.

Finishing a rim

To finish the rim of a pinched shape, it is best to wait until the shape has firmed to become leather-hard. Then, to level it, cut the edge with a knife tip or grate it down with a surform blade.

Once the rim is level, pare the section of the rim with a hacksaw blade to even it out. You can choose if you want to pare a round, flat or tapered rim once it is level and of a uniform thickness. (See also page 48, rims and edges.)

Evening out the wall

1. To even out the surface of the walls of your pinched shape, use a serated kidney first, followed by a smooth, metal kidney on the insides of a curved shape. To pare down any thick or high points, see also page 47, making a wall smooth and even.

2. To even out the surface on the undersides of your curved shape, use a hacksaw blade to pare down any thick or high points, followed by a smooth, metal kidney. Wiping the clay with a damp sponge will remove the marks left by the hacksaw blade.

Using a pinched shape as a starting point

Grafting coils onto a pinched, open shape is an ideal way to make a bowl.

1. Leave a fat edge to give a good fixing surface for the coil. The thick seam can be thinned down once the join has been made. Thoroughly score and slurry the first coil into position to make a strong join and then smear down the coil, both inside and outside, onto the pinched cup shape. Continue to coil and pinch the coils to the height that you require (see page 42, coiling techniques).

2. Walls, joins and pinchmarks can be pared and thinned with the use of a hacksaw blade and a metal kidney, supporting the wall when applying pressure with such tools with the non-working hand. Resting the shape in the lap provides soft support while doing this, and is a comfortable way of working (see pages 47 and 48 for how to finish the wall and rim). The clay can be worked in this way while the work remains plastic, but any final finishing should be left until it has become leather-hard.

To make a hollow, enclosed shape by pinching, see the bottle project (page 69).

COILING TECHNIQUES

Coiling is a fast, versatile method of constructing large or small, complicated or simple, clay forms. The technique allows the freedom to make imaginative, unrestricted forms that are built up in a series of stages. It is important to have a clear idea of the finished shape before you start to coil, so a preliminary drawing will help to determine how to start and where to change direction as the work progresses. It is useful to remember that coils of clay can be grafted onto any piece of leather-hard clay-work that has been formed using a different technique.

It is quite usual to continue to work on a coiled piece for a number of sittings, interspersed with waits while the work becomes firm enough to carry on. To continue a piece over a number of working sessions, it must be wrapped in polythene to keep it airtight and leather-hard so that it is still workable when you return to it. A paint-stripper is a useful tool (see page 37, tools) to speed up the drying and waiting times. The gun should be kept on the move to prevent any areas of clay becoming overly dry. Once the clay has gone beyond the leather-hard stage and starts to show the characteristic, pale colour of dry clay, work can no longer continue. The coils will not join and the walls will be hard and too brittle to work. It must be discarded and thrown into the reclaim bucket to start afresh.

Some makers prefer not to pare away the pinchmarks or to join the seams of each coil – everyone has their own particular style of making and attaching coils. You can choose whether to have a textured or smooth surface, or a wall that is thick or thin.

Making coils

1. To roll out a coil, start by squeezing out prepared plastic clay.

2. Allow plenty of room on your working surface so that the coil can be turned over on itself fully. Use the length of your fingers to apply pressure where the coil is thick.

Coils can be made in bulk and can then be stored in plastic, or else can be rolled out as you move along with the work. Coils do not have to be rolled: flattened strips can also be used to build a clay wall.

When joining circuits of coils to build up a wall, it is helpful to turn the work on a banding wheel (see page 37, tools). Tear or cut your coils to the correct length for the shape as you lay each one into place. Use coils that are soft enough to join without having to apply unnecessary pressure, which could distort a soft, supporting wall.

Joining on the first coil

To coil onto a flat base of plastic or leather-hard clay, join the first coil to the top of the base. It is a good idea to slurry and score along the attaching edge of the first coil, as well as the base, to knit the clay together well.

Grafting onto leather-hard clay formed by another method

To start to coil onto the top edge of a curved base that is leather-hard, score and slurry the first coil and the top edge to make a thorough join.

Grafting onto an existing piece of leather-hard clay

To start to coil onto an existing piece of leather-hard work made by an alternative method, score and slurry the adjoining surface and the first coil to make a thorough join.

Coiling

As you continue to coil, it is unnecessary to score and slurry soft coils onto one another. But if the work has been left to firm to leather-hard to allow for a change of direction, then score and slurry to join the next coil to the leather-hard clay.

To join a coil once it has been laid in place, smear down clay from the upper coil onto the base or coil below it along the entire seam line. Do this on both the inner and outer face of the wall. As you smear the coil down onto the wall or base, support the wall with your other hand so that the applied pressure does not move the wall out of alignment. Make the strokes rhythmical and of a consistent pressure to keep the wall under control as it begins to grow. When you are coiling, allow the work to firm to leather-hard as you progress as it must be able to support the weight and pressure required to join the next coil. If the wall is soft, it will be unable to support the applied weight, causing the shape to sag, crack or collapse.

If the join seams of each coil are required to show on the outer face of the wall, it is sufficient to join from the inside wall only.

Changes in direction

Changes in direction are particular points at which the piece should be allowed to firm before continuing to work.

If you want to achieve a shape that is straight or vertical, place and join the coils directly on top of each other.

If you want to direct a wall outwards, place and join the coils to the outer edge of the coil below.

If you want to direct a wall inwards, place and join the coils to the inner edge of the coil below.

45

To bring the shape out on an edge, pinch the coil to lengthen it.

You can even and reinforce the inside of a curved wall while it is still plastic using the curved edge of a serrated kidney (see page 37, tools) on the inside of the curve. This will also help to strengthen the coil joins.

The toothed edge of a hacksaw blade will even and reinforce an external wall. Alter the direction and angle of the tool in your hand to avoid causing flat ridges. Use sweeping motions, and reinforce by crossing your previous strokes diagonally.

Once you have joined each coil, pinch or pull it up while it is still soft. This will give each coil more height, as well as making your work lighter. To make a paper-thin wall, it is easier and quicker to use the thickest coil that the supporting edge will take, and to pinch it as far as the clay will allow.

Making a wall smooth and even

If you want to achieve a smooth, even or paper-thin wall, allow the clay to become leather-hard before paring the wall. Apply pressure with a smooth, metal kidney, using the curved edge for the inside of a curved wall and the straight edge for the outside. You can bend the metal kidney as you make the sweeping strokes to prevent flat ridges from occurring. To smooth a straight-sided wall, use a hacksaw blade to pare the wall down to an even surface.

If you are working on an enclosed form that is narrower than the width of your hand, smooth and finalise the surface after joining, smearing and pinching up each coil. This will avoid having to go back to work inside the narrow shape. Manoeuvring tools on the internal walls of a narrow shape once the coils are built is awkward, and sometimes impossible.

Checking the shape

Every time that you add a coil, check its shape and direction to ensure that it is where you want it to be. Turn it on the banding wheel as you inspect its side in profile. Get a bird's-eye view and check the top profile, too. If your shape is wayward, you can alter it as follows to bring it under control.

A bulge or an uneven profile can be altered by making 'V'-shaped cuts to bring the shape in. Slurry and score the cut on both meeting edges to join them back together or, if they are still soft and thick enough, smear them back together. An additional small piece of soft clay, slurried and scored over the join, can give added reinforcement to the joined area if it feels weak. Once the join has firmed, it can be pared down. A wall shape or slight depression that is still plastic can be eased out by using a stroking pressure with the fingertips.

Rims and edges

1. Wait for your rim or top edge to become leather-hard before using a surform to level it. Bring your eyes level with the edge or rim to see where you need to apply pressure with the surform blade.

2. To create an even section to the rim, pare it where it is thickest, using a hacksaw blade. Apply pressure wherever the section is thickest, until you have made it uniform along its entire length.

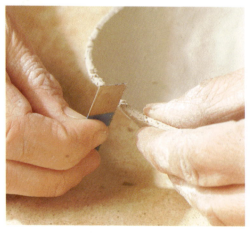

3. Continue to use the hacksaw blade to shape the evened rim to a flat, rounded or tapered edge.

4. You can remove any unwanted tool marks with a damp sponge.

SLAB-BUILDING

Slabs or sheets of clay can be worked in two different ways to create work that is either straight-sided or has a softer, curved feel. Straight walls require a leather-hard slab, while curved walls require the slab to be soft enough to bend without cracking. To make clay slabs, use well-prepared clay (see page 17) that is soft enough to move freely, but not so wet that it sticks to your hands or rolling pin.

Rolling out a slab

To roll out a slab or sheet of clay, work on a wooden board or a cloth that has been pulled taut. Any creases in the cloth will make creases in your finished slab, creating a potential fault line along which your finished work might crack. Choose a pair of slats (see page 37, tools) of the same thickness that are suitable for the size and weight of the work that you are preparing to make.

1. Press out the clay with the heel of your hand, spreading it as far as it will go. Standing up will help to push your weight down, onto the clay, to make this part of the process easier.

2. Aim to roll out your slab to the same thickness throughout. Using rolling slats to guide the rolling pin will help you to achieve this. Rest the rolling-pin ends on the slats and start to roll from the centre outwards. Exert pressure on the rolling pin at the points where the clay is higher than the slats and continue doing this until the clay will not move out any further. Allow a pocket of air back under the clay by lifting the clay. Pick it up by peeling up the edges first. You will find that this pocket of air will enable the sheet of clay to be spread out again. Carry on rolling in different directions with the rolling pin until you have attained the required thickness.

To wire-cut slabs

1. Prepare a block of clay (see page 17, clay preparation) and knock it into a solid block.

2. Pull the harp through the block of clay, holding the ends of the harp firmly on the surface while dragging it through the clay.

3. Move the wire up one notch at a time to slice the entire block. Separate the slabs after cutting them by putting them on separate boards or sandwiching them between sheets of newspaper.

Tip While your slabs are soft and laid flat on a board, you could print texture into their surface. For an example of this technique, see the hump-mould-bowl project on page 89.

Bringing flat slabs to leather-hard and storing them

1. Slabs have a tendency to curl at the corners and edges as they firm up to leather-hard. To avoid this, firm up your slabs slowly and weigh them down with flat, wooden boards. Slabs can be interfaced with newspaper and stacked up to four high, then weighed down. Put any larger slabs under smaller ones so that they all remain flat. Better still, if you have sufficient boards and space, put each slab under a separate board.

2. While the slabs are firming up, ensure that they are not becoming too dry to use. As soon as they can stand on their edges without flopping over, retain them at this leather-hard stage until you are ready to use them. Lay down a sheet of polythene and stack up the slabs, with a sheet of newspaper between each touching face. Bring the polythene over the stack to create an airtight cover. Some newspaper on the top slab will absorb any condensation inside the polythene. The stack can then be weighted down with a board on the top. If you leave them overnight, the slabs will even out to the same consistency. This is beneficial when joining them together on a piece of work as they will all shrink at the same rate, reducing the strain on the joined seams.

Tip Leather-hard slabs are ideal for straight-sided precision. Leather-hard clay can be scraped, pierced and cleanly cut.

Planning ahead for leather-hard slabbing

Make all of your slabs in one go at least a day before you use them to allow time for them to become leather-hard. Work out how many slabs you will need and what size to make. Roll them out to a slightly bigger size than you need because the slabs will be trimmed as you use them, and because the edges of the slabs tend to dry before the central area. Make a couple of spares in case you make a mistake while cutting.

Choose a clay that will have a low shrinkage rate. That means a grogged or sandy clay that reduces the risk of work pulling apart at the seams (see page 14).

Cutting, joining and cleaning seams

To find out how to join and cut leather-hard slabs, see the lidded-box project (page 83).

Soft-slabbing

When using soft slabs, it is unnecessary to prepare the slabs in advance as they can be rolled as you need each piece. If the work that you intend to make is going to be high-walled or very curved, then you may need to leave the slabs on a board until they are firm enough to stand, but soft enough to bend. You will have to gauge the correct time to use them. Cut them roughly to the height that you want and hold them on their edges to see if they will stand and curve as required.

To prevent your soft-slab-work looking fingermarked, any cleaning and trimming is best done when the work has firmed up to leather-hard. Likewise, if you wish to add more slabs to a wall to build up its height, wait for the initial wall to become firm enough to support the weight of any further slabs that you apply to the top edge. Wait again for the clay to firm before finishing the top edge or rim.

PRESS-MOULDING

The moulds used when working with the press-moulded-clay technique are made from a porous material, such as plaster or biscuit-fired clay (see page 236). The porosity of the mould removes moisture from the clay, allowing it to come away from the surface of the mould without distortion. Plaster (or plaster of Paris) is an inexpensive material that is used to make moulds. When plaster is mixed with water and allowed to set and dry, it becomes a porous material that takes up water like a hard sponge. This property is useful when pressing and moulding clay-work. There are various types of plaster sold by ceramic suppliers and good builders' merchants, and note that 'special' and 'slow' plasters provide the porosity necessary for press-moulding.

Pressing sheets or pieces of clay into, or over, a mould is a technique that is used to repeat identical shapes with relative ease. Hollow or drop moulds are used to press out the under face of a press-moulded piece, while hump moulds are used to press out the upper face (see page 89, the hump-mould-bowl project). Inlaid or textured slabs are ideal for the hump or draped working method, which is used to press out the upper face. A coiled or separately moulded foot-ring can be joined to a soft shape while it rests on the hump mould.

The pressed shapes can be used either as starting points or as components. Little skill is needed to fill press moulds, which can be used repetitively to create shapes for decorating or to make components that can be joined. Decorative pieces of shaped or textured clay that are joined to the clay surface, known as sprigs, are also made in press moulds (see page 103, the relief-tile project).

The porosity of the mould removes moisture from the clay, allowing it to come away from the surface of the mould without being distorted.

Mould-making tools

EQUIPMENT

1 **Mask:** plaster-like glaze materials create dust, so inhalation should be avoided by wearing a mask.

2 **Plastic bucket:** for mixing plaster.

3 **Flexible plastic sheet:** for containing plaster when it is poured for casting.

4 **Bench-scraper:** for cleaning work surfaces and equipment.

5 **Bristle brush and sponge:** for applying soft soap for 'facing-up' plaster as a separating agent.

6 **Coping saw:** to cut profile-formers.

7 **Profile-formers:** to shape clay models.

8 **Surform blade:** to pare sharp corners on cast plaster.

9 **Rubber mallet:** for muted, sharp taps to release set plaster.

10 **Shock-absorber weight:** to disperse mallet blows to plaster.

11 **String, builder's strap and parcel tape:** for securing side sets.

12 **Wet-and-dry paper:** for the final smoothing of the plaster surface.

13 **Rubber kidney:** to finalise a press-moulded surface.

Pressed shapes are removed from plaster or biscuit-fired clay moulds (see page 236) once the clay has firmed to the leather-hard stage.

If a shape is removed from a mould while it is firm, but still soft enough to move without cracking, it can be distorted or tapped to take on a new shape.

Once trimmed and cleaned, further additions of clay, such handles or decorative sprigs, be applied to the shape. Such additions can give variety to repeated shape.

Symmetrical shapes formed in a mould can be joined together while leather-hard to make an enclosed form.

Press moulds can be filled with different-coloured clays, or shaped pieces of clay, which can be arrange and joined to make a pattern or texture.

Using a hollow or drop mould

1. A rolled slab of plastic clay is laid into the hollow mould. The slab is eased into place using a damp sponge to prevent the fingers from indenting the soft clay.

2. Any folds or doubling-up of the clay slab can be evened away using serrated and smooth, metal kidneys. A flexible rubber kidney (see page 55, tools) can be used to add a final finish to the surface of the clay.

3. The edges can be trimmed level with the edge of the mould or they can be left to overhang it, allowing enough clearance for the clay to be removed from the mould without locking around the edges. The clay shape is removed from the mould once it is leather-hard.

Making and designing a plaster mould

Models for making press moulds (see page 59) can be thrown as a solid shape on the wheel or can be carefully modelled or sledged using clay. Casts can also be taken of such objects as shells or plastic toys to make press moulds, adapting them for any undercuts using plastic clay. (See page 103, relief-tile project.) The clay-model-making method shown in this book requires fewer steps when forming shapes to make moulds than methods used when making models from plaster. Plaster is used to make models when greater precision is required.

When plaster is used to produce a mould by pouring it into, or over, a shape, the plaster sets solid. Because of this, each wall of every part of the model except the top one must be tapered (this is called draft), allowing the mould to be withdrawn from the model. Draft also allows the press clay to be withdrawn from the mould. Any undercuts caused by indents or changes in direction that do not take this draft into consideration must be removed or modified by adapting the model so that it does not lock into the plaster once it has set.

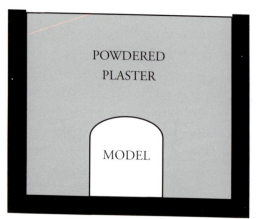

COTTLE WALL

POWDERED
PLASTER

MODEL

BOARD
OR BASE SET

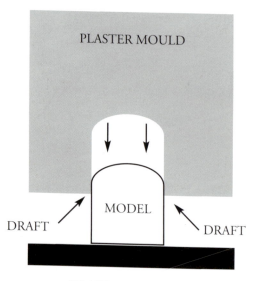

PLASTER MOULD

MODEL

DRAFT

DRAFT

BOARD OR BASE SET

Making and designing a plaster mould

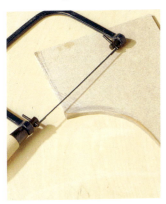

1. Use thin plywood and a coping saw to cut your required shape to make a profile-former. Cut the shape to be continuous and smooth in its line. Angle-cut the wood along the edge of the cut shape.

2. A flat, smooth board about 1–2cm thick is used as the 'base set' of the mould. The base set acts as a guide to the notched former, which is pulled along the edge of the base set to shape the soft clay. The cottle wall must be solidly secured into place about 3–5cm away from the edge of the model. To do this, planning is required before starting a model to ensure that the shape and size of the supporting board or base set is correct. The base set also provides a guide against which to rest the base edge of the cottle wall at a 90° angle to the board. It will ultimately provide a neater finish for your mould.

3. Build up soft clay to roughly the shape of your model.

4. Draw the notch of the profile-former along the edge of the base set. As you do this, remove any soft clay that is too high, and add soft clay where it is too low. This is called sledging.

5. Finish off any indents or small lumps by hand until the surface of the model is good enough to cast.

6. A rubber kidney is useful for making a final surface at this stage.

7. Secure a wall of bendable plastic or linoleum (this is called the cottle wall) around the edge of the base set, being careful not to damage the model. (Smooth wood can be used for straight-sided moulds.) Seal the base with a thick coil of clay and tape around the girth of the walls with strong parcel tape.

8. Look at the area to be poured and place your estimated volume of water (see page 24, step 4) into a clean plastic bucket. Gradually scatter plaster into the water until it forms a peak on the surface of the water.

9. Leave the peak to soak up water for one or two minutes before stirring the plaster and water into a smooth mix with your hand. Try not to pull air down into the mix as you do so. Continue to stir until the plaster begins to feel thicker. At this point, it is ready to be poured.

Tip The cottle wall must be well secured to avoid any leaks or falling walls caused by the pressure of the weight of the plaster as it is poured inside the retaining walls. Secure straight-sided walls with a builder's strap or tightened string around the outside of the retaining wall.

10. Mix enough plaster to cover the clay model completely, to about 3–4cm above the top of the model. Pour the plaster over the model inside the cottle wall. Pour the plaster mix quickly against the inner side of the cottle to prevent air bubbles from being pulled into the cast. Before the plaster sets, give the supporting board or table some sharp taps to force any air bubbles in the plaster mix to the surface of the mould. Move any leftover plaster in the mixing bucket to a bin with a rubber kidney, then wash out the plaster residue in the bucket before it sets.

11. Allow the plaster to become hot before removing the cottle wall and the clay model. Any clay that has been used for the model or for securing the wall should be kept separate from your clay-work clay. Use it again only for mould-making work. This is because plaster that finds its way into a wall of a finished piece of work can cause a firing fault called a 'blow out'.

12. Clean up the sharp corners of the mould with a surform blade.

13. Remove the clay model using a wooden modelling tool.

14. When plaster is cast into, or against, plaster, as is the case when making hump moulds, a separating agent must be applied to the surfaces of the plaster. Soft soap (called 'English crown soap' in the USA) dissolved to a thin liquid in warm water is used to seal a plaster surface before having plaster poured against it. Soft soap is available from ceramic suppliers. Other separating agents include petroleum jelly or oil, which are useful when separating plaster from plastic objects or wooden surfaces.

15. Mix the soft soap to a thin, soapy texture using hot water.

17. Repeat the process some 10 to 12 times with two sponges until a gloss appears on the plaster surface. Casting plaster up against another plaster face is called 'running plaster'. It is important that the set plaster piece is wet before 'facing up' with soft soap. If the mould has been left to dry, soak it in water for at least 10 to 15 minutes.

18. Remove any soap suds or water droplets before pouring the mixed plaster into the hollow mould to make the hump mould.

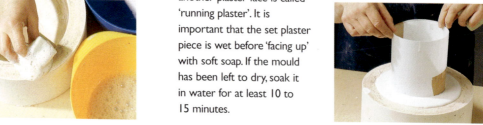

16. Apply the liquid soft soap thoroughly with a sponge and allow it to soak into the plaster for around 15 seconds. Remove any excess suds with a damp sponge.

19. Place a collar of flexible plastic or lino in the centre of the setting hump mould.

20. Slop in the remaining plaster to cast the foot of the hump mould.

21. Scrape the plaster with a sharp, straight tool to level it out while it is still soft, but just beginning to set.

22. The sharp corners of the cast mould can be filed away using a surform blade.

23. When the mould parts are set, put them into a sink and let cold water run onto the parting line for about five minutes. Put a metal weight against the mould-part sides and tap the weight with a rubber mallet. Repeat this around the sides to send dispersed shocks through the plaster parts until you detect movement of the parting line or until the tone of the tap changes. This will indicate that the plaster is going to be released.

24. At this point, the moulds can be pulled apart. The surface of the plaster mould can be sanded smooth with wet-and-dry, Carborundum paper. Any plaster breakages can be repaired with polystyrene cement (such as UHU in the UK).

Tip Allow the moulds to dry before using them. Place them on their sides in a warm place, with air circulating around them. Moulds should be stored in a dry place, as should bags of plaster, as any moisture will reduce their strength and will shorten the plaster's setting time. Plaster moulds should be stored in a separate area from one in which clay-based activities are taking place. The working moulds should be handled with care when in contact with clay, particularly when trimming the edges of pressed shapes with a knife.

MODELLING AND BAS RELIEF

Long before clay was used to make vessels, it was used to model human and animal figurines to try to ensure, by sympathetic magic, fertility, or the continuity and increase of grain crops.

It is often easier to make a figurative or sculptural piece as a solid form. Soft clay can be built up by joining soft pieces of clay to soft clay with gentle pressure or a smearing action. Soft clay can also be built up onto previously firmed or leather-hard clay, but be sure to attach the first soft pieces by scoring and slurrying them into place. To achieve a sharp, crisp finish to modelled clay, allow the work to become leather-hard first. It can then be worked with tools to carve it into a more refined surface. (See page 93, modelled-figure project.)

When building a solid form, the clay shape must be scooped out or hollowed once it has firmed and before it becomes dry. This enables the water in the clay to escape as the work is heated in the kiln, and prevents it from exploding as a result of the pressure of the evaporating water or steam. Thick forms should be fired slowly during the initial stages of the biscuit-firing until the kiln has reached red heat or 600°C.

The following section explains the correct procedure for hollowing out solid, or bas relief, clay forms.

1. A solid form can be cut with a knife when it is leather-hard. Wait until it is at this stage so that the shape does not distort as you cut it. Cutting a solid figure open like this allows you easy access to all parts of the solid model with the hollowing-out tool.

2. Once it has become leather-hard, a solid form can be scooped out using a looped-wire modelling tool (see page 37, tools). Should the tool work its way through the wall, any holes made can easily be patched. Using the same clay, score and slurry the patch into place and smear it down.

3. Leave some thickness of edge on the wall so that there is enough surface area to rejoin the pieces together again by slurring and scoring.

Modelling and hollowing bas relief

1. Modelled- or joined-clay bas relief that is thicker than approximately 2cm can be hollowed or scooped out from the back once the work has firmed to the required consistency.

2. Hollowing out from the back using a hooped tool is necessary to reduce the thickness of the wall for drying and firing purposes.

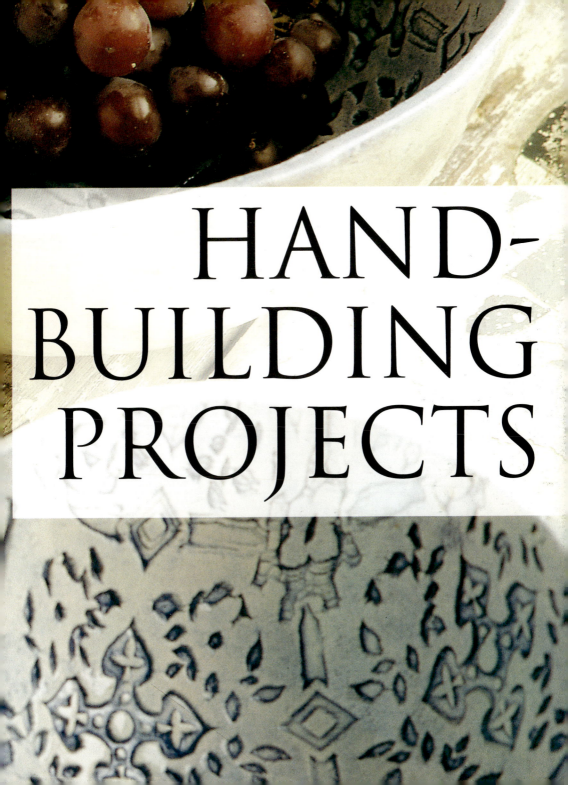

HAND-
BUILDING
PROJECTS

PINCHED-BOTTLE PROJECT

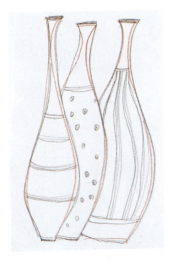

This pinching project sets out to make a set of bottles that work well as a group. Two pinched-cup shapes can be joined together to make a sealed, hollow sphere that can then be altered while soft into another shape. The air trapped inside the sphere prevents it from collapsing inwards while it is being gently tapped or beaten into the shape required. This technique of beating the shape is called 'paddling'.

To find out about the pinching technique, refer to the hand-building section (page 38). To find out how these bottles are decorated, go to page 163, and to find out how they are glazed, go to pages 214 to 215.

The clay used is white earthstone.

1. Pinch out two cup shapes that are elongated.

2. Gather in the clay at the wall to keep the shape narrow. Leave a level, fat rim on both shapes to allow for the next step. Make the second cup slightly larger so that it overhangs the first.

3. While they are still soft, place the cup rims together and pull or smear one edge over the other. The larger, second cup is pulled over the edge of the first to make a complete seal. Smear or pull the clay around the entire circuit of the seam line. When this is done, the air trapped inside the enclosed shape will keep it inflated like a balloon.

4. Once it has been completely sealed, the enclosed, hollow shape can be tapped, rolled or paddled to finalise the form. If the seal is not complete, it will distort itself by buckling inwards or deflating. If you detect a hole or weak point, seal it straightaway with very soft clay before going any further.

5. Make a small hole with a needle to allow some of the internal volume of air to escape. This will prevent the shape from cracking as it shrinks. Allow the paddled shape to firm to leather-hard.

6. Finish the lower section of the bottle, evening out the base. Do this now, as once the neck has been made, the bottle will be too unstable to turn over. Use the serrated edge of a hacksaw blade to pare the surface, to even the wall and to finalise the shape.

7. Tool marks can be removed with a smooth kidney. To do this, it is often more comfortable to rest the work in your lap.

8. Score and slurry the top of the shape.

9. Apply a first coil to build the neck of the bottle.

10. Join the clay all of the way around, both inside and outside the coil. Once it has been thoroughly joined, pinch up the height of the coil. You can work on more than one piece at a time and can alternate between each bottle to ensure that the work is firm enough to support the weight of more added coils of clay.

11. Continue to coil the neck to the required height and shape (see page 45).

12. Trim the rim level with a knife tip and allow the neck to firm.

13. Finish the entire surface, using the serrated side of a hacksaw blade to pare and even the wall.

14. Use a metal kidney to smooth away any tool marks.

15. Finish the rim by levelling it with a surform blade.

16. Even its section with a hacksaw blade. Then shape the rim, finally wiping away any tool marks with a damp sponge.

Once the bottles are bone dry, they can be biscuit-fired to 1,000°C.

COILING PROJECT

This project sets out to make a figurative piece using the technique of coiling. A preliminary drawing is made to work out the scale, the points of change of direction and the shape of the base. Before each point at which the direction changes, the work is put aside to firm to leather-hard so that it can support the next layer of clay when it is joined without collapsing. To find out how the bird is carved and glazed, go to pages 167 and 217. For information on how to roll, join and pinch out coils, refer to pages 42 to 46.

The clay that was used for this project was white earthstone original.

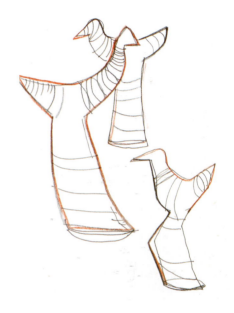

1. Roll out a clay sheet and draw out the size and shape of the base.

2. Attach the first coil to the base by scoring and slurrying it into place.

3. Pinch up the first coil in the direction of the legs, squeezing the wall together where you want the wall to lean inwards and pinching out the coil to lengthen it where you want the coil to lean outwards. Keep the wall straight where it needs to be upright.

4. Once you have attached the first coil, you can trim away the excess clay from the base.

5. Continue to coil for about three coils, then stop and allow the work to firm.

6. Continue to apply coils until the next change of direction, roughly where the legs first bend.

6a. If you need to bring the coils inwards as your work progresses upwards, make 'V'-shaped nips and tucks while the clay is still soft.

6b. Alternatively, you could double-over the wall, smearing the clay wall back together to remove the seam, thereby bringing the direction of the wall inwards.

7. Allow the coils to firm before applying the coils for the last change of direction.

8. When the clay has firmed, continue to coil to the tops of the legs. Make sure that the tops of the legs are wide enough to support the fixing of coils and the distributed weight of the body of the bird.

9. Much of the finishing work of the leg section can be done now, before leaving the legs to become sufficiently leather-hard to take the weight of the bird's coiled body. Pare down the surface using the serrated edge of a piece of hacksaw blade.

10. Attach the first coil to the tops of the legs in the direction in which you want the body to start off. Score and slurry the soft coils into position thoroughly as the leg section is leather-hard. Pinch out the height of the coil once it is attached.

11. Continue to coil the body, waiting for each section to firm before the wall changes in direction. Bring the top of the bird's body inwards by placing each coil inside the last one. While the clay is still soft, you can also make 'V'-shaped cuts to bring the wall in further.

12. Allow the main body to firm well before starting on the neck. Score and slurry the first coil of the neck thoroughly to join it onto the main body, which is leather-hard. Pinch up the first coil in the direction that you want to take it. You can use a wooden modelling tool to join the coils on the inside if you cannot get your finger inside the narrow opening. Continue to coil the neck, stopping every two or three coils to allow the clay to firm.

13. Allow the neck to firm before making the head.

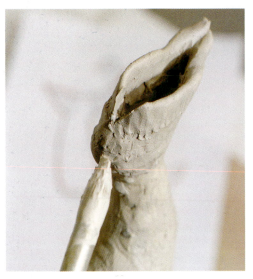

14. Add coils at the back of the head to bring the shape over the head only.

15. Shorten each coil to bring the beak to a point.

16. Score and slurry the final coil for the head into place, smearing the clay together on the outside.

Once the bird is bone dry, it can be biscuit-fired to a temperature of 1,000ºC.

SOFT-SLAB-DISH PROJECT

This dish has been planned to be built using rolled, soft slabs of clay. The slabs are rolled out in sheets, then cut into strips. Inlaid, coloured clay has been rolled into the slabs while they were still soft. To see how the clay is inlaid, see page 168. The strips are chamfer-cut before positioning them in place to splay the sides of the dish. To see how the dish is glazed, go to page 226.

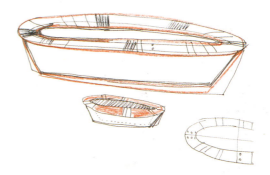

The clay used to make this dish is buff grogged with red-and-white clay inlay.

1. Start by rolling out a flat sheet of clay that is slightly larger than the finished size required. Compress the base sheet with a metal kidney before joining any walls to prevent weak points from forming cracks. A sprinkling of sand on the board will also assist the shrinkage as it will help to prevent the base sheet from sticking to the board. Mark out on the sheet of clay where the walls are to be placed.

2. Take your strip of clay and lay it in line with the edge of your worktop or board. Take a ruler and place it 1 or 2cm away from the edge of the clay.

3. Holding the knife at an angle, chamfer-cut the edge of the strip along its length.

4. Score and slurry this first strip into place, giving it a slight wiggle as you push it on to knit it firmly together with the base.

5. Overlap the next end of the wall and then angle-cut along its length.

6. This will form a neat join and will also increase the surface area that can be scored and slurried for joining.

7. Remove any excess slurry from the strip of clay with a soft, wet paintbrush or else a sponge.

8. Butt the next strip (which you should cut to the same height and chamfer-cut in the same way as the first) to the first wall, having made an angle-cut to its end. Score and slurry all of the touching edges of the base of the strip and the first wall to attach them thoroughly.

9. Continue to make up the circuits of the walls, joining each strip in the same way.

10. Run a surform blade along the top edge of the leather-hard walls to the angle at which you wish to attach the top strips. Keep the angle at which you hold the surform blade constant.

11. Thoroughly join each cut strip of inlaid clay to the top edges of the wall by scoring it into place.

12. Smooth the edges with a hacksaw blade.

13. Run a surform blade along the top edge of the leather-hard walls to the angle at which you wish to attach the top strips. Keep the angle at which you hold the surform bade constant. In doing this, you can also level the tops of each wall.

14. Thoroughly join each cut strip of inlaid clay to the top edges of the wall by scoring it into place.

15. Continue joining the strips.

The dish is left to become bone dry before biscuit-firing it to approximately 1,000°C.

LEATHER-HARD-SLAB-BOX PROJECT

This lidded-box project is designed to show the use of leather-hard slabs to make a straight-sided object. To find out to how to roll out even slabs or sheets of clay and to take them to a consistency ready to make a straight-sided object, see pages 50 to 52. You will need to prepare all of your slabs in advance to make this project. Seven slabs are needed as two are used to make the lid. Roll out each piece slightly larger than the finished sides as there will be a little wastage with this technique (see page 22, reclaiming or reconstituting clay). Once it has been joined and finished, the box will be painted and drawn into. To find out more about this technique, called 'sgraffito', see pages 170 to 171.

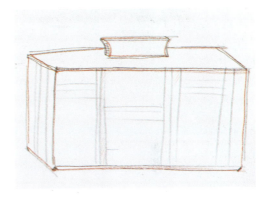

Tip   If you have never joined slabs before, see the chapter on joining, which starts on page 26.

The clay used to make this box is crank.

1. Take the prepared leather-hard slab that you plan to use as your base and draw out where the walls are to be placed on it.

2. Cut the first wall with a straight edge.

3. Join the straight edge to the top face of the base by scoring and slurrying it into place.

4. Cut the second adjoining wall straight along its bottom edge, and at a 90° angle, cut along its side edge. Score and slurry it into place.

5. As you join each slab, remove the excess slurry with a square-ended tool.

6. Repeat the above steps for the third wall.

7. Do not try to slot the last wall of the box between the first and the third wall because it is probable that the fit will be insufficient to obtain a good join or a good fit. Butt the fourth wall to the side of the first wall and the end of the third wall.

8. Once all of the slabs are joined, trim the excess off the joins with a knife and finish the joins with a hacksaw blade, wiping the seams together with sweeping strokes so as not to pull the joins apart.

9. To clean and trim the base edge, drag the box to overhang the edge of the board on which it is sitting in order to reach this area with the tools.

10. Trim the top of the walls level using a surform. To do this, move your head so that your eyes are level with the top edge.

11. Join one of the lid slabs to the levelled top edge.

12. Trim back the edge.

13. Mark out the lid opening before cutting it out. Hold the knife against a straight edge at an angle that tilts outwards to cut the lid out.

14. Remove this angle-cut piece carefully, without distorting its shape, and fix it to the centre of the second lid slab, top side down, scoring and slurrying it into place.

15. Clean away any excess slurry using a flat-headed modelling tool.

16. Replace the joined lid into the slot in the lid opening so that the fit is flat, and trim the second top piece to the exact size of the box.

17. If you have cleared away all of the slurry on the lid, dragging a hacksaw blade down the sides of the lid and box to create an exact fit will not cause the lid to stick.

17a. Once your lid has been cleaned up and trimmed to the exact size of your box, it should look like this.

18. Wrap the box in polythene and weight the lid before leaving it overnight.

19. The next day, cut the pieces of the handle and then join them together.

20. Trim the excess off the pieces of the handle with a knife, hacksaw blade and smooth, metal kidney.

21. Once the joined handle pieces have firmed, level the base of the handle with a surform blade.

22. Unwrap the box and attach the handle to the lid by slurrying it and scoring it into place.

Once the box is bone
it can be biscuit-fired
temperature of 1,000
Fire it with its lid in
so that it does not wa
during firing to a diff
shape to the lid fitting
Biscuit-fire it on sand
help the base to move
it shrinks and so prev
the base from crackin
it does so.

HUMP-MOULD-BOWL
PROJECT

This project was designed to show the process of press-moulding using a hump mould. This type of press-moulding allows a decorative texture or surface to be added to the upper face of the bowl. To see how the mould is made, go to pages 58 to 63. To see how the clay sheets are textured, see page 164. To see how the biscuit-fired bowls are glazed, go to page 222.

The clay used to make these bowls was white grogged 1,020–1,140ºC.

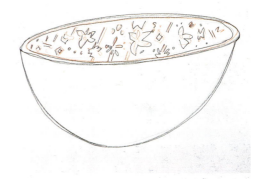

1. Lift the textured slab carefully onto the mould.

2. Ease the slab in place over the mould using a damp sponge to prevent your fingers from indenting the soft clay.

3. Where the slab overlaps the mould, pare away the excess clay with the serrated edge of a hacksaw blade.

4. Trim back the edges of the rim with a knife or cutting harp. You can use the edge of the mould on which to rest the tool to get it level.

5. Smooth the surface using a rubber kidney.

6. Leave the work until it is sufficiently firm to lift off the mould.

7. Lift it off before it becomes too dry to prevent the bowl from cracking when it shrinks.

8. Once the bowl has been turned over, you can even and shape the rim by using a surform blade to level it off.

9. Finally, use a hacksaw blade and sponge to finish and clean up the rim.

Once the bowl is bone dry, it can be biscuit-fired to a temperature of 1,000°C.

MODELLED-FIGURE PROJECT

Modelled or joined clay is hollowed or scooped out once it has firmed to a leather-hard consistency. This is necessary to reduce the thickness of the wall for drying and firing purposes. This figurative project is designed to show how this is done. To see how this figure is glazed, go to page 218.

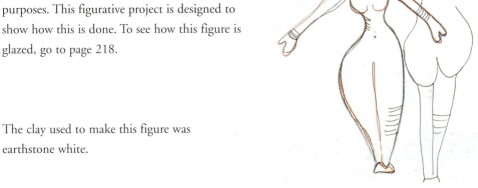

The clay used to make this figure was earthstone white.

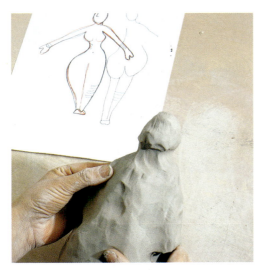

1. Start the figure by squeezing out the shape from a soft piece of clay.

2. Roughly shape the figure into your desired form, referring to your initial drawing as you do so.

3. Use tools or your hands to pull and push the clay to where it is needed.

4. While the clay is still soft, you can attach soft pieces of clay where the figure needs to be built up. Soft clay can be joined to soft clay by applying pressure with your fingers or tools while you continue to build and model the figure. Once the clay has become leather-hard, it is necessary to score and slurry to build up the surface.

5. A piece of hacksaw blade is useful to take away clay from the shape when you need to move or rearrange it. Lay down the figure on your work surface and leave it while it firms to leather-hard.

6. When the figure is firm enough to turn it over, attach clay by scoring and slurrying the back of the figure.

7. Use your fingers and wooden modelling tools to compress the clay and form the shape that you require.

8. Wrap the parts that will dry the fastest in thin polythene to stop them from becoming too dry to work.

9. Finish the surface of the model once the figure has firmed to leather-hard.

10. A sharp, crisp finish can be achieved using modelling tools or a hacksaw blade, followed by a wipe with a damp sponge.

11. Once you have completed work on the shape and surface of the figure, it is ready to hollow out. Cut the model down its middle while it is still leather-hard.

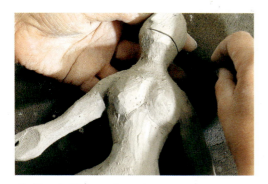

12. Cut the figure at the neck.

13. This gives tools access to scoop out the head.

14. Use a hooped-wire tool to scoop out a little clay at a time without changing the external shape.

15. You can protect the figure while you do the scooping-out work by resting it on a pad or sponge.

16. Rejoin the parts by scoring and slurrying.

17. Wiggle the pieces together so that they knit together well.

18. Make the seam disappear using a hacksaw blade and by scoring in and slurrying soft clay wherever it is necessary.

Once it is bone dry, the figure is biscuit-fired at a temperature of 1,000ºC.

MODELLING-BEADS PROJECT

This project demonstrates how to colour clays using stains or oxides. It is followed through in the glazing and firing sections to show how to fire small objects that cannot be placed on a kiln shelf. (See page 216 for glazing and page 241 for firing.)

The clay used for this project is porcelain. You can colour any light or white clay by kneading in oxides or commercial stains.

To work out how much colour to add with a repeatable formula, you can use the following calculation on the understanding that approximately 30 per cent of plastic clay is water:

150g of wet clay = 100g of dry clay.

Weigh your clay to calculate its dry weight and then weigh your stain or oxide to achieve the percentage addition of colour that you desire. Stains and oxides vary in strength, so it is a good idea to test the percentage additions by firing them to their required temperature before going ahead with large batches or making the finished work. You will need anything from 1 to 2 per cent, for a light to strong blue in a pure-white clay using cobalt oxide, through to 10 per cent, for a black clay using a commercial stain.

In this project, 10 per cent grass-green stain is used to colour the green clay for the leaf beads. Black porcelain is used to make the spacer beads by kneading in 10 per cent black stain.

Wear a mask when weighing any dried materials as it is not advisable to breathe in airborne particles of colouring oxides.

1. Weigh the clay or oxide.

2. Moisten the stain or oxide before kneading it into your clay to help to distribute the colour evenly and to minimise airborne particles.

3. As you knead the clay, check that the colour is being evenly distributed.

4. Once your clay has been prepared, pinch out the leaf-shaped beads using your finger and thumb, leaving a fat end that can be pinched out.

5. Once the beads have been pinched and shaped ...

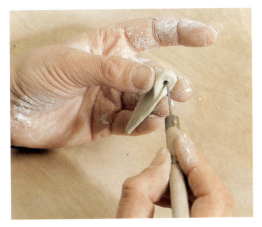

6. ... they are ready for a hole to be pushed through them with a needle.

7. Roll different-shaped beads to act as spacers on the thread.

8. Pierce a hole in these beads, too.

9. Once all of the beads have firmed enough to be handled without being squashed, use a knife to pare the porcelain into shape.

10. By working the beads at this leather-hard stage, you can achieve a cleaner look for the porcelain.

11. Leave the beads to dry. At this stage, porcelain can be sponged or filed using a plastic mesh to refine the shape and surface still further.

When the final cleaning work has been finished and the beads are bone dry, they can be biscuit-fired, sitting on a kiln shelf, to a temperature of 1,000ºC.

RELIEF-TILE PROJECT

This project shows the use of sprig moulds to create texture. Found objects are used for the moulds to recreate the shapes as raised pieces of clay that are attached to the leather-hard clay surface. Go to pages 165 to 166 to see how the sprigs are removed from the moulds. See page 225 for the final finishing of the textured surfaces. The clay used for this project was red clay and crank clay, mixed 50/50, which created a good, open clay to prevent the tiles from warping as they dried.

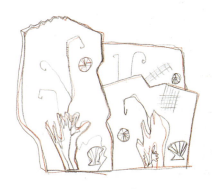

To make the sprig moulds

1. A sheet of clay is rolled out to a sufficient thickness to sink the found objects to their halfway seam lines. Objects that will be released from the moulds because they do not have any under-cuts have been chosen for this project.

2. A cottle wall is placed around the objects and clay sheets to prepare for pouring the plaster moulds. A little oil is painted onto each object to act as a separating agent, which helps to release the objects once the plaster has set.

3. The plaster is poured inside the cottle wall so that it covers the found object by about 3cm. The plaster is left to set. The moulds are trimmed of sharp corners with a surform blade and left to dry for a few days before they are ready to take a pressing to make the sprigs.

To make the tiles

1. Drawn lines are made by pressing string into the surface of the clay. Folded fabric is rolled into the clay to create a lined texture, and a piece of plastic mesh gives more texture to the design. The tiles were rolled to an approximate thickness of 1cm to help to prevent them from warping.

2. The objects are removed from the soft tile to leave indented impressions in the clay surface.

3. Pressings are taken from the sprig moulds and left to become leather-hard before being joined to the tile.

4. The clay pieces are arranged in position before each is attached to the tile surface by scoring and slurrying both touching surfaces. Any excess slurry is removed with a wet paintbrush once the sprig has been attached. See page 166 for further tips on attaching sprigs.

5. The tiles are cut to shape by overlapping the clay and cutting the top and bottom pieces together.

Once the tiles and attached pieces are leather-hard, the back of the tile panel is scooped out using a hooped modelling tool. This is to lessen the thickness of the clay so that it can be fired safely without the risk of wet clay on the inside forcing the tile apart in the kiln (see pages 64 and 65). Dry the tiles slowly so that they do not warp. Once they are bone dry, they are biscuit-fired to a temperature of 1,000°C. Biscuit-fire the tiles on sand to help them to move as they shrink and so prevent cracking.

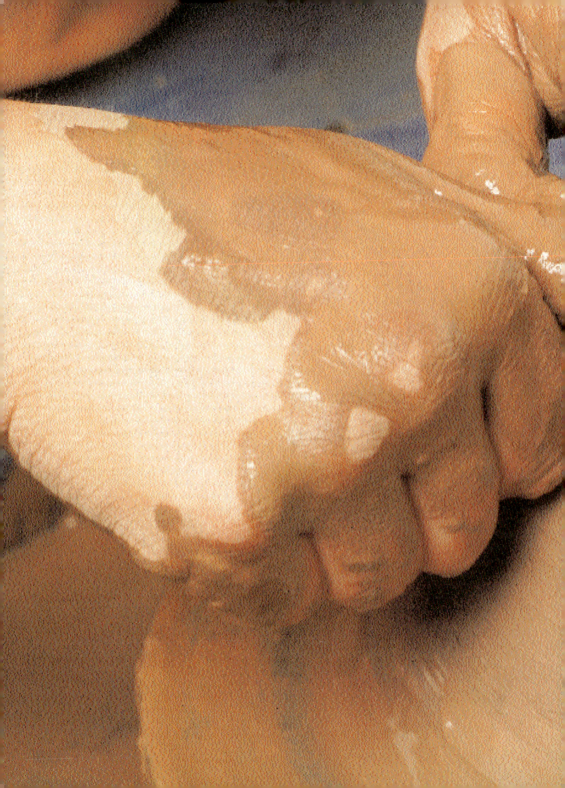

THROWING

Once you have mastered the technique of centring and pulling up the

clay wall, it is then possible to start to channel more attention into

planning the shape or form of your thrown work. When you set out

to learn to throw, you quickly understand that centrifugal force

automatically makes the clay move outwards. Making a bowl or a

plate is relatively easy, so start with a cylinder! When you are able to

throw a cylinder with a thin, even, 90° wall, you will know that you

are in control of the clay (not the other way around!)

THROWING TOOLS

1 **Wires, twisted and smooth:** for cutting thrown shapes from the wheelhead.

2 **Angled knife or bamboo tool:** for making a clean-angled base edge and an angled notch into which to slide the cutting wire or twisted cotton.

3 **Needle:** to cut top edges level while throwing, and to test the thickness of a base section.

4 **Sponge:** to remove surplus water from the inside of a shape.

5 **Chamois leather or thin polythene:** for compressing rims.

6 **Bats:** circular wooden bats are used for throwing large or open ware. These are positioned on the wheelhead by means of a thrown pad and corresponding holes and pins on the wheelhead.

7 **Board:** to place work on after throwing.

8 **Callipers:** for measuring widths of galleries, lids and other fitted shapes.

9 **Dottle:** to remove water from the inside base of a tall, narrow, enclosed shape.

10 **Ribs:** for applying pressure while throwing.

11 **Toggle and twisted cotton:** for cutting lids and small objects off a hump when throwing.

12 **Turning tools:** for turning leather-hard work.

13 **Metal kidney:** to pare and smooth walls.

14 **Hole-cutter:** for cutting circular holes for teapot lids or straining holes.

15 **Stiff brush:** for scoring and applying slurry.

16 **Knife:** for cutting.

UNDERSTANDING YOUR HAND

If you are a beginner, equip yourself with everything that you need before sitting down to start. Make up 10 to 20 orange-sized pieces of clay (see page 17, clay preparation) so that you have plenty to practise with. The essential things that you need in order to learn to centre and throw a cylinder are: lots of water, a wire for cutting, a sponge, an angled knife or bamboo tool, a needle and a piece of chamois leather or thin polythene.

Everyone throws slightly differently – for example, some people open out with their thumbs, while others use their forefingers. Do what feels comfortable and what works for you.

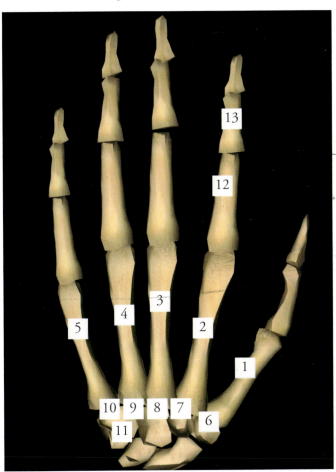

Some techniques refer to specific bones, so please use this diagram for reference.

1 First metacarpal.
2 Second metacarpal.
3 Third metacarpal.
4 Fourth metacarpal.
5 Fifth metacarpal.
6 Trapezium bone.
7 Trapeziod bone.
8 Capitate bone.
9 Hanate bone.
10 Triquetrim bone.
11 Pisiform bone.

THROWING A CYLINDER
Centring clay on a wheelhead

Speed is important in order to be able to centre clay. Ensure that the clay is always wet, so that your hands do not stick to the clay, by repeatedly throwing water onto the ball or wall whenever you feel the clay becoming dry. If you are working on a kick wheel, ensure that the wheel is turning in an anti-clockwise direction. If you are learning to throw, use a smooth clay as a grogged clay can cause abrasions on the sides of your hands.

Because the clay is turning, you do not have to cover the whole area of the clay with your hands – it will come into your hands as you keep them still. Imagine a clockface on the ball of clay as you sit facing it on the wheel. Your hands stay at 3 o'clock and 6 o'clock to do all of the work required. When you are throwing, your two hands are always working together as a team – never separately!

WHEEL STILL

WHEEL MAXIMUM SPEED

1. Start by slapping the clay ball onto the centre of the dry wheelhead.

2. Pick up a handful of water and throw it over the ball of clay, turning the wheel to maximum speed. Cup your hands on the outside of the ball, using the flat, metacarpal areas on the sides at 3 o'clock and 9 o'clock, bringing the metacarpal and trapezium bone over the top to flatten it out using pressure on both sides of the ball. Do this while bringing your elbows into the sides of your body. Resting your elbows on the edge of the wheel, try to keep your arms in a fixed position.

3. With the wheel at maximum speed, keep your arms locked steady and tucked into your body, and your elbows on the tray. Use both your right and left fifth metacarpals to exert pressure on the ball as you move them up the sides to the top, forcing the clay into a tall column.

WHEEL MAXIMUM SPEED

4. Once the clay is in a tall column, bring your right hand over the top, keeping the flat metacarpals of your left hand at 6 o'clock on the outside of the column. Working out from the centre to 3 o'clock, move the side of your fifth metacarpal around to 6 o'clock on the top of the ball, while exerting pressure downwards. At the same time, exert pressure at 6 o'clock on the side with your left hand. Push the weight of your body forwards and down on the top, and keep your arms locked into your body. Force the column down, against your left hand, into a flat-topped, flat-sided shape.

WHEEL MAXIMUM SPEED

5. Repeat these last two steps if the clay does not feel centred. This has to be spot-on before proceeding any further. If your hands or arms are moving in the slightest way from side to side, then the clay is not centred.

WHEEL MAXIMUM SPEED

111

Opening out the base

WHEEL MEDIUM SPEED

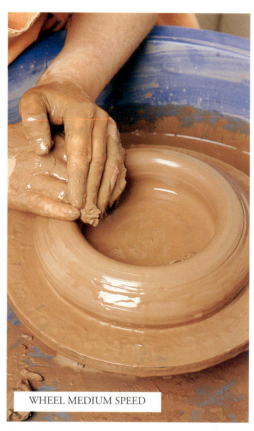

WHEEL MEDIUM SPEED

1. To make a flat base, and with the wheel turning at a medium speed, keep your left hand at 6 o'clock, with the trapezium bent over the top to keep the shape under control. Using the fore-finger or thumb of your right hand, and starting at the central top point, exert pressure to make a hole within 4–5mm of the wheelhead. Keep your hands linked or touching as you do this.

2. With the wheel still at medium speed, keep your left hand at 6 o'clock, with the trapezium bone over the top edge to support the outside wall and top edge. Drag your right finger or thumb towards you, level with the bottom of the hole, while exerting steady pressure against the wall to make a flat base that is level. You can only drag the base open as wide as the initially centred clay is spread. If you go past this point, a ring of clay will come away from the base.

3. The wheel should still be turning at a medium speed. Pulling out the base often throws the centred clay a little off-centre, even though the left hand acts to keep it under control. You now have to recentre the clay before proceeding any further, while at the same time positioning the clay ready for pulling up the wall. First, make a notch at the base of the clay with your thumb as the wheel turns. Next, move the clay into an industrial-chimney shape by putting the tip of your left forefinger down, inside the wall, at 3 o'clock and resting your thumb on the top edge. Position your right-hand thumb on top or touching your left thumb and bend the second knuckle of your forefinger (between the second middle phalanx and the second proximal phalanx) into the notch that you have made with your thumb. When you have found this position and you have your elbows locked into your body and/or on the wheel tray, use the side of your second proximal-phalanx bone to nudge the wall back into the centre, against the side of your left forefinger. Keep control of the top edge with your thumbs as you do this. Make a conscious effort to lean the neck inwards, and to make a sharp corner on the inside at the bottom with the tip of your left forefinger.

WHEEL MEDIUM SPEED

Pulling up the wall

WHEEL SLOW SPEED

WHEEL SLOW SPEED

1. With the wheel turning at a slow speed, hold the forefinger and thumb of your left hand so that their tips touch the inner and outer wall at 3 o'clock, and scoop a handful of water onto the first and second metacarpal area. It will then run down and wet the inner and outer walls at the same time.

2. To distribute the clay evenly along the wall to the maximum height that you can achieve, you will have to repeat this process three or four times, with the wheel turning slowly. First, make a notch with your thumb in which to put your right knuckle, using your thumb along the outside of the bottom of the base.

WHEEL SLOW SPEED

3. Position yourself with the tip of the forefinger of your left hand in the inside corner at 3 o'clock, and your thumb on top. Put your right-hand second knuckle into the notch at 3 o'clock and touch the thumb of this hand against your left thumb to contain the top edge.

4. Using slight pressure, squeeze your knuckle and fingertip together to get hold of a wave of clay, which you should then move up the wall to the top edge. The wheel should still be turning slowly.

WHEEL SPEED SLOW

WHEEL SPEED SLOW

WHEEL SPEED SLOW

5. Use the side of each hand to support the wall as you do this, keeping your arms locked into the sides of your body. Don't stop halfway and apply pressure in one place, or the top part of the wall will come away in your hand. (And remember to breathe while you are doing this!)

6. Don't be tempted to follow the clay around the wall, but continue to repeat this procedure while remaining at 3 o'clock, and at a slow speed, making a conscious effort to bring up the wall in an industrial-chimney shape, with the neck narrowing at the top.

115

7. With the wheel turning slowly, remove the pressure gently each time that you reach the top edge. Compress the top with your thumb just before you move your hands away. If the rim begins to grow higher in one place, you can trim it back using a needle. Position your right elbow steady on the wheel tray, then the tip of your left forefinger inside the top rim at 3 o'clock. Holding the needle steady with your right hand, move it in to meet your left fingertip. When the ring has been cut through, lift it off and compress the rim again.

8. Now that you have distributed the clay evenly throughout the wall, you can straighten up the wall to make a cylinder. Do this by using the outside edge of your left forefinger to push out the inside wall in the places where it leans in. Lean back to see the profile so that you can see where it needs to be pushed further. You can use a fingertip or a rib to support the push and prevent it from coming out too far. Remember to keep working at 3 o'clock, with the wheel turning at a slow speed.

Removing the work

1. Before taking the cylinder off the wheel, which should still be moving at a slow speed, you must remove all of the water on the inside to prevent the base from cracking as it dries. Hold your arm steady and reach down with a small sponge to the inside base as the wheel turns slowly. Soak up the water and squeeze out the sponge, repeating this process until the water has been removed. If you cannot get your hand inside, then use a sponge on a stick (a dottle, see page 108).

WHEEL SLOW SPEED

WHEEL SLOW SPEED

WHEEL SLOW SPEED

2. As the wheel continues to turn slowly, finish the rim with a wet piece of chamois or a wet, thin piece of polythene. Flop it over the rim at 3 o'clock and pull it down by holding it on the inner and outer side. You can remove excess slurry in this way, too.

3. Run a rib or flat tool against the slowly turning sides to remove the throwing slurry. Doing this will dry the sides sufficiently to enable you to pick the cylinder off the wheelhead once you have cut the base.

WHEEL SLOW SPEED

4. With the wheel still moving slowly, cut an angled notch with a knife or bamboo tool around the base. Hold the knife or bamboo tool at 3 o'clock, and at a 30° angle to the wall to direct the clay away from the soft clay wall. The cutting wire will fit into this notch, and will make a neat finish to the base of the cylinder.

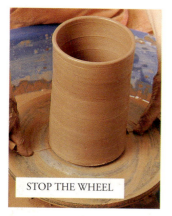

STOP THE WHEEL

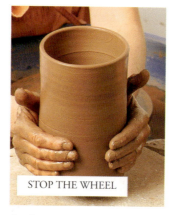

STOP THE WHEEL

5. Stop the wheel. Now cut through the base of the cylinder, holding the wire taut and pressing down on the wheelhead.

6. Scrape dry your hands along the bottom edge of the wheelhead or the corner of a board and gently place them around the cylinder, below the centre of gravity. Removing the slurry from your palms and the sides of the cylinder produces sufficient friction to lift it safely onto a board.

Cylinder wall section.

Don't be scared to push your skill forward by distributing the clay evenly along the wall to make your work as light as possible.

Keep the pad of clay left by the cutting wire dry. You can slap the next piece of clay onto it to continue working. If it is wet, the next piece will not stick.

THROWING A BOWL

When you start to throw a bowl, open out the clay with a centre point and pull up the walls without flattening out the base (unless you want a flat-based bowl). What you are aiming for is the same curve on both the inside and the outside of the wall. If you want to turn a foot-ring out of your bowl once it has become leather-hard, remember to allow for the extra clay needed to support the bottom of the curve of the bowl, which will be removed at the turning stage.

Fixing a wheel bat to throw a bowl or a plate

Lifting medium to large bowls off the wheelhead is hard to do without distorting them. In order to lift off a thrown bowl, fix a bat to the wheelhead in the following way. You can use this pad again and again to throw a succession of works as long as you keep it damp. Recut the channels if they start to disappear.

WHEEL MAXIMUM SPEED

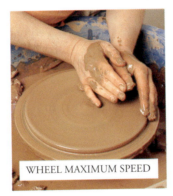

WHEEL MAXIMUM SPEED

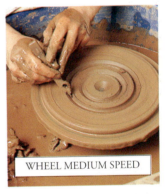

WHEEL MEDIUM SPEED

1. With the wheel turning at a fast speed, centre a piece of clay about the size of a grapefruit on it. As you bring the tall column down, spread it ...

2. ... so that it is wide and level, using the heel of your right hand and then your fingertips, or the flat edge of a rib.

3. Set the wheel turning at a medium speed. Use an angled knife or bamboo tool to cut three or four circular channels out of the clay.

WHEEL STOPPED

4. Stop the wheel. Now cut four to six channels across the circles. These will allow the air to escape, creating suction that will hold the bat in place. Dampen the level top of the grooved pad and wiggle the bat while applying pressure. This should be sufficient to hold the bat in place. Test to ensure that the bat is stuck down before you start to throw.

Throwing a bowl

WHEEL MAXIMUM SPEED

WHEEL MAXIMUM SPEED

Stop the wheel and slap your prepared clay onto the centre of the dry bat. Set the wheel turning at a fast speed. Centre the clay, bringing it down from the tall column to roughly the width of the foot of the bowl that you would like to make.

1. With the wheel still turning fast, open up the centre with your thumb or forefinger, supporting the outside wall and top edge with your left hand. Bring the opening hole down to about 1–1.5cm away from the top of the bat (depending on how much clay you want to turn out to make your foot-ring). Squeeze your outside and inside fingers together at the base to make a fat, rounded ring.

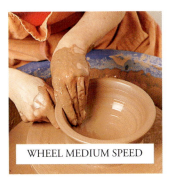

WHEEL MEDIUM SPEED

WHEEL SLOW SPEED

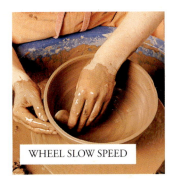

WHEEL SLOW SPEED

2. Set the wheel speed to medium. Starting at the bottom, move a wave of clay upwards, with your hands positioned at 3 o'clock. As you do this, concentrate on forming a curve on the inside with your left-hand fingertips. Leave plenty of clay in the rim at this stage.

3. Set the wheel speed to slow. Continue to create the inside curve and to distribute the clay up to the rim.

4. Once the clay has been distributed, use your fingers or a curved throwing rib against the supporting fingers of your right hand gently to press out a smooth curve on the inside shape that should sweep continuously from the inside centre to the inside rim edge.

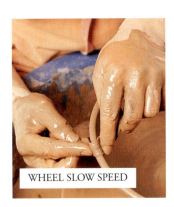

WHEEL SLOW SPEED

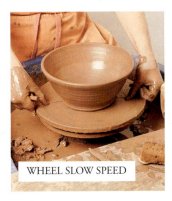

WHEEL SLOW SPEED

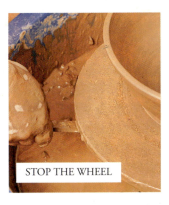

STOP THE WHEEL

5. Finish the rim by compressing it into the shape that you want – rounded, square or tapered – using some chamois or polythene.

6. Remove any excess water and slurry with a sponge or a throwing rib. Cut a notch at the base, then stop the wheel before cutting under the base with a taut wire.

7. Lift the bat carefully, using the handle of your knife or a bamboo tool as a lever to remove it from the pad.

121

Turning a foot-ring

To turn the foot-ring of a bowl or similar item, you must first allow it to firm to leather-hard. The ideal time is after it is firm enough to sit on its rim without damaging it, and when you can apply pressure with the turning tools without the foot buckling. To get it to the correct stage at the top and bottom, remove the bowl from its bat and allow it to firm to leather-hard while sitting on its rim. It is hard to say exactly how long this should take, as it will depend on the room temperature and the circulation of air around the object. Keep a close eye on the drying process: if you allow the bowl to dry for too long (i.e., when the clay has turned lighter in colour), then you have left it too late for turning.

Look at the bowl before you start to turn it to gauge how much clay you can remove. Feel the weight in your hand and the thickness of the wall between your fingers. Remember that you are aiming for a curve on the outside that matches the curve on the inside of the bowl. You should not have to turn the area of the rim edge at all to achieve this. To assess the weight distribution again, remove the bowl from the wheelhead and pick it up to feel it. If it is still too heavy or thick, reposition it with lugs and continue to turn more clay away.

WHEEL SLOW SPEED

1. Place the bowl on its rim on the wheelhead, using the rings as a guide to centre it. Run a damp sponge over the wheelhead area around the rim as you turn it slowly. Once it has been centred, stop the wheel and take three fat lugs of plastic clay. Push each one down at equal spaces apart, trapping the rim as you smear them down without smearing clay onto the bowl. The damp wheelhead will hold the lugs and bowl in place.

WHEEL SLOW TO MEDIUM SPEED

2. Set the wheel at slow to medium. Remembering the curve on the inside of the bowl, use your nail to mark the size and thickness that you are aiming for before turning the foot-ring.

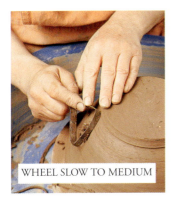

WHEEL SLOW TO MEDIUM

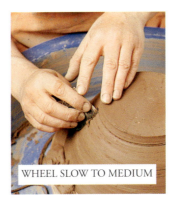

WHEEL SLOW TO MEDIUM

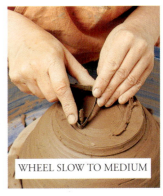

WHEEL SLOW TO MEDIUM

3. With a turning tool, take the outside clay away first, following your memory of the inside curve.

4. A tap on the wall can help a practiced ear to gauge the remaining thickness before too much is turned away. If in doubt, stop and take the bowl off the wheelhead to feel how much clay is left.

5. Once the outside shape is how you want it, begin to turn out the centre of the foot-ring, using the turning tools.

WHEEL SLOW TO MEDIUM

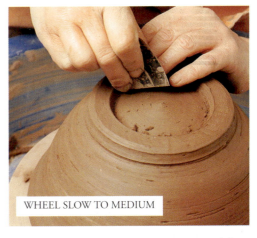

WHEEL SLOW TO MEDIUM

6. Shape the inside of the foot-ring in a way that suits the curve, shape and distributed weight of the overall shape.

7. Leaning away from the bowl every now and then to view its profile will help you to make an informed assessment of its overall shape.

Throwing a plate

Throwing a plate is similar to throwing the pad on which to sit a wooden bat, in that the clay must be spread flat. The difference when making a plate is that the extra clay required to make the rim of the plate is spread out from the centre to create a thick rim that is pulled out as the last step.

WHEEL MAXIMUM SPEED

WHEEL MAXIMUM SPEED

1. With the wheel turning at the maximum speed, place enough clay on the bat to spread out to the finished size of your plate. Centre it and spread the clay, using the heel of your hand and then the little-finger side of your hand, moving it from the centre outwards, through 3 o'clock and down to 6 o'clock.

2. Pull out the clay using your fingertips or thumb, spreading it to the outside edge to form a thick, rounded ring. Start from the centre and drag the clay towards you, moving your hands towards 6 o'clock. Make the base flat and level, to a thickness of about 6mm, unless you want to turn out a foot-ring, in which case it should be thicker.

WHEEL MEDIUM SPEED

WHEEL SLOW TO MEDIUM

3. Set the wheel to turn at a medium speed. Compress the round, fat rim on the edge to recentre the clay, and then compress the centre of the plate, moving your flattened fingertips in, from 6 o'clock to the centre, and then back out again to even it out. (The flat edge of a throwing rib is also good for performing this step, and removes the throwing slurry at the same time.)

4. Set the wheel to turn at a medium to slow speed. Working at 3 o'clock, pull out the rim by first making a notch at the base of the outside edge in which to fit a right-hand knuckle or fingertip.

5. Finally, set the wheel to turn slowly. Fully direct the wall in the direction in which you want the rim to be once the clay has been distributed evenly by applying gentle pressure with your fingertips to lift or drop the rim down.

WHEEL SLOW SPEED

Turning a plate

1. Once the plate is leather-hard, it can be placed, rim facing downwards, on the wheelhead for turning. Fix it to the wheelhead using three lugs of clay.

2. Turn the outside shape first to follow the inside curve of the plate.

3. Then turn the inside of the foot-ring. To do this, the clay must be firm enough to enable you to exert pressure over the big expanse of the base.

4. Move the turning tools from the foot edge to the centre and back again. The flat edge of a metal kidney is useful for the final finish when turning out the base of a plate.

Throwing lids

There are many solutions to lid-making. Some lids sit on an inner shelf called a gallery, while on other fittings the gallery is on the lid itself. A sunken lid that has galleries on both the lid and the pot is often used for teapots to prevent the lid from falling out when the pot is tipped for pouring (see the lid fitting in the teapot project, pages 136 to 139).

The secret of making a lid that fits is to measure the aperture before any shrinkage has taken place, i.e., when it has been freshly removed from the wheelhead. Larger lids can be thrown individually off the wheelhead and smaller lids off a hump of clay. The latter method is advantageous when throwing small lids as it is easier to get your fingers underneath to pull out the curve on the wheel – there is also less clay to turn away. Step-by-step photographs for the hump method are shown in the following section. And the method for a wheelhead-thrown lid is shown in the teapot project starting on page 132. Most lids require turning at the leather-hard stage to remove excess clay and to neaten them off before attaching a knob or a handle. (To see how to split a rim to make a drop gallery and measure its aperture, look at the teapot project.) Lids should be dried and fired sitting in their aperture or position on the pot. Like this, lids and pots shrink and move together to make a good final fit. (See page 219 to 220 to find out how the lid fitting of the teapot is wiped clean of glaze, then set in the firing to prevent it from sticking.)

A lid fitting sitting on a gallery.

Another example of a lid fitting sitting on a gallery.

A ginger-jar lid.

A lid fitting with no gallery.

Examples of some different types of lid fittings.

Throwing a lid off a hump

WHEEL MAXIMUM SPEED

WHEEL MAXIMUM SPEED

1. Centre a grapefruit-sized, or larger, piece of clay. It is sufficient for lid-throwing purposes just to centre the top section of the hump. Make a neck near the top, using pressure with your fingertips at a point that allows sufficient clay to pull out your lid.

2. Push a finger down, into the middle of the centred top, to the depth of your lid. Use the side of your right forefinger to keep the clay centred as you do this. Pull out the lid to the shape and size that you require, stretching or trimming it to fit the required aperture. Use callipers with the points facing in to measure how far to pull out the clay.

WHEEL MEDIUM SPEED

3. Leave enough thickness of clay to split into two with a needle held steady at 3 o'clock.

WHEEL MEDIUM SPEED

4. Push the flange down with a flat-ended tool.

WHEEL SPEED SLOW

5. If the lid is too large, trim it with a needle or a wire held taut. If it is too small, pull out the clay from the centre.

WHEEL MEDIUM SLOW

6. Fit the thread of your twisted-cotton-cutter into the notch as you turn the wheelhead at a medium–slow speed and wait for it to wrap into the notch. With a fast-flick wrist action, pull the cotton thread to make a straight cut through the notched, narrow neck.

STOP THE WHEEL

7. Lift the lid off the hump with two fingers and set it on a board. Leave it to become leather-hard before turning it.

THROWING
PROJECTS

THROWING-A-
TEAPOT PROJECT

Making a teapot is a test of designing skill as the lid, handle and
spout must feel as one when they are fitted together. The base of
this teapot is quite narrow; its body shape is rounded. This shape
will help to circulate the tea in the pot as it brews. To make this
shape, keep the neck in when pulling up the walls and leave
enough clay to split the rim at the end stage in order to make
the gallery on which to sit the lid. Distribute the clay evenly
throughout the body – this curved shape should not require any
turning at the leather-hard stage. To see how this teapot is
glazed, go to page 219.

The clay used to make this teapot was red earthenware.

1. Attach a bat to the
    wheelhead (see pages 119 to
    120) and centre your
    prepared clay (see page 110).
    With the wheel turning
    quickly, spread the clay to
    roughly the size of your base.

WHEEL MAXIMUM SPEED

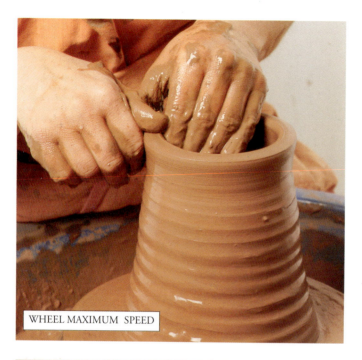

WHEEL MAXIMUM SPEED

2. Pull up the walls into an industrial-chimney shape, leaning the neck inwards in order to keep control of the shape. Leave a thick rim so that there is enough clay spare at the end to split the rim.

WHEEL MEDIUM SPEED

3. Once you have distributed the clay while making the height of the wall, switch the speed to medium. Push the shoulder down by supporting with your left hand while pushing down with your right hand.

WHEEL MEDIUM SLOW

WHEEL MEDIUM SPEED

4. Belly out the side of the pot by exerting gentle pressure with your fingertips from the inside. With the wheel turning at a medium to slow speed, ease out the belly to make a smooth transition in the curve.

5. Set the wheel turning at a medium speed. Now split the fat rim with a needle.

6. Push down the inner gallery with a flat-headed tool. Finish the rim with a piece of wet chamois leather or else some thin polythene.

WHEEL MEDIUM SPEED

135

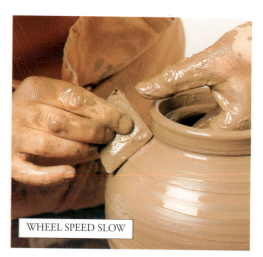

WHEEL SPEED SLOW

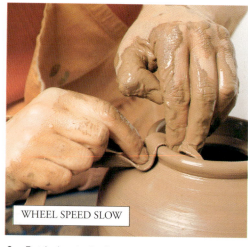

WHEEL SPEED SLOW

7. With the wheel turning slowly, finalise the curve of the body with a throwing rib, supporting the rib with your fingers from the inside.

8. Finish the rim by flopping a piece of wet chamois leather or wet plastic over the rim and squeezing gently on each side. Finish the bottom edge with an angled cut made with a knife or a bamboo tool. Cut under the base of the body with a taut wire and lift the bat off the wheelhead.

9. Measure the size of the gallery as soon as you have finished the body, before any shrinkage has taken place. Measure the diameter of the lid aperture and, keeping the callipers fixed, transfer them to a ruler. Throw the lid with the inside curve or shape in keeping with the design of the body. Measure the lid with callipers, the points facing inwards. Trim the lid with a needle if it is too large. If it is too small, pull out the clay a bit more.

Making the lid

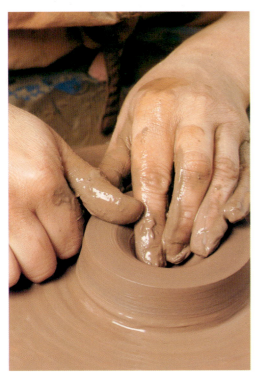

1. Put your clay on the dry wheelhead or bat to throw your lid. Slap the clay into the centre, then turn the wheel fast. Pull up sufficient clay to make a lid with a flange. Throw the lid upside down, as though you were making a bowl with a fat rim.

2. Split the rim with a needle.

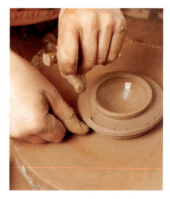

3. Push down the flange with a flat-ended tool.

4. Measure the lid with callipers, with the points facing inwards, and stretch or trim the lid to the correct size. Ensure that the measurements correspond to the measurements of the body of the teapot.

5. Trim or extend the lid to the correct size. Remove any water with a sponge. Cut the lid off the wheelhead with a taut wire. Wait for the lid to become leather-hard before turning it on the wheelhead.

Turning the lid

1. Centre the lid and fix it in place with three lugs.

2. Turn the lid to make a shape that suits the teapot body.

3. While it is still on the wheelhead, score and slurry the centre.

4. Attach a round ball of very soft clay. Drop some water onto the ball in preparation for throwing the knob into your required shape.

5. Set the wheel to a fast–medium speed. Shape the clay by centring it first and applying pressure with your fingertips to bring it into the required shape.

6. Finally, cut a hole in the teapot lid to allow the air to escape as the tea is poured. (If this hole is not cut, the tea will 'glug' as it is poured.)

Making the spout

First refer to pages 128 to 129, throwing a lid off a hump.

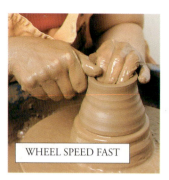

WHEEL SPEED FAST

WHEEL SPEED MEDIUM

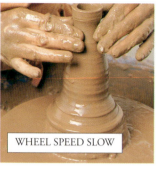

WHEEL SPEED SLOW

1. Recentre enough of the top of the hump to throw a small industrial-chimney shape, distributing the clay evenly up its wall with the wheel turning fast. Make an undercut notch at the base of the chimney with an angled knife or bamboo tool.

2. Set the wheel speed to medium and lift the chimney into a narrow-necked, curved, tapering shape.

3. Set the wheel to slow and use four fingers to 'collar' the neck in further as you move your fingers upwards from its waist.

WHEEL SPEED SLOW

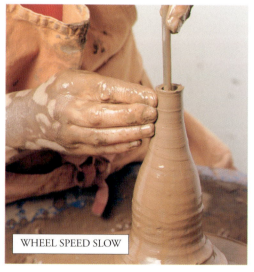

WHEEL SPEED SLOW

4. Move your fingers to the top edge, leaving the base as a wide, flared 'skirt'.

5. Use a paintbrush handle or rounded stick to support the inside of the spout's neck while exerting gentle pressure upwards to lengthen, narrow and thin the wall of the tip further.

WHEEL SPEED SLOW

6. Remove the throwing slurry from the outside of the spout with a curved throwing rib or else a metal kidney.

7. Trim the top of the spout with a needle.

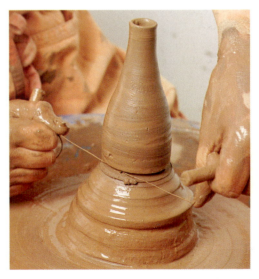

8. Compress the end of the spout with a chamois leather or thin piece of polythene.

9. Flat-cut through the base of the spout with a wire at the point of the undercut angled notch and move it to a board to become leather-hard.

Assembling the teapot parts

Before assembling your teapot components, it is advisable to wrap them together in polythene and to leave them overnight. Doing this will ensure that all of the pieces firm to the same degree of leather-hardness, and that they will consequently shrink at the same rate.

1. Put the lid in place before attaching the spout to enable you to judge the overall look of the joined parts as they come together. Pick up the spout and hold it behind the body to see where to make the diagonal cut that will leave the flared skirt uncut at one edge. The top of the spout must be at least level with the top of the teapot body. If it is not, you will not be able to fill the teapot with liquid without the spout overflowing.

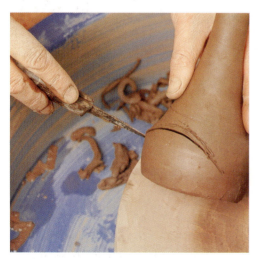

2. Mark the line to cut with a knife tip, moving around the curve of the teapot body.

3. Cut the spout as marked, and angle the cut edge to fit snugly around the shape of the curve.

4. Hold the cut spout against the body and mark around it.

5. Remove the spout again and cut holes inside the marked lines indicating where the spout is to join the body. The area of the holes cut should be at least twice that of the exit of the spout, so that there is sufficient liquid pressure for the tea to pour smoothly into a cup.

6. Score and slurry both the spout's attaching edge and the marked area around the straining holes that you have cut.

7. Clean and smooth the clay around the attached area to match it visually with the teapot body.

8. Join a handle (see page 153, pulling a handle) directly in line with the spout. Start by joining the top part of the handle by scoring and slurrying the attaching area of the body and the handle in line with the spout. Give the handle a slight wiggle to knit the joining areas together.

9. It is important that the handle is still soft enough to bend without cracking in order to bring it into position with a curve before joining it at its base end.

10. Angle-cut the joining ends of the handle to sweep upwards and then flow into the body of the teapot at the bottom end. Remove any excess slurry and score marks at the joining areas with a damp sponge and/or a soft paintbrush.

11. The teapot body must be leather-hard in order to join both the handle and the spout to it. It must be firm enough to support the weight of both, but wet enough that the handle does not crack at the join as it dries.

Allow the teapot to dry slowly to become bone dry before biscuit-firing it at 1,000°C. Put the lid in place and leave it there while it dries and fires so that the lid and pot shrink and move together to make a good final fit.

T H R O W I N G - A - J U G   P R O J E C T

In throwing terms, this jug is basically a cylinder with a swollen belly. Pull out the throat and lip while it is wet on the wheelhead, then join the handle once the jug has firmed to leather-hard. Give the jug enough 'throat' to channel the poured liquid over the lip. A jug is a symbol of generosity, so combine the handle and body to make one whole to give this feel. To see how this jug is glazed, go to page 227.

The clay used to make this jug was red earthenware.

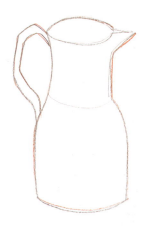

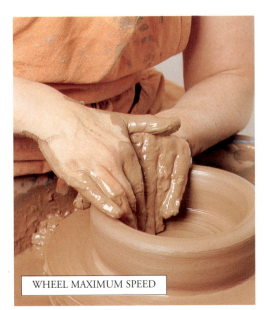

WHEEL MAXIMUM SPEED

WHEEL MEDIUM SPEED

1. With the wheel speed set to fast, centre the clay on a bat and open out the base to the size of your imagined or drawn design (see page 112).

2. Switch the speed to medium and pull up the clay wall, keeping the neck in all of the way and distributing the clay evenly up the wall.

WHEEL SPEED MEDIUM

3. This shape should not require turning to remove any excess clay or weight.

WHEEL SPEED MEDIUM

4. Slow down the wheel to ease out the belly from the inside. Use your left-hand fingertips to exert gentle pressure where you require the jug body to swell, supporting the wall with your right hand, or with a throwing rib, as you do so. Stop the wheel and lean back to see the profile of the shape that you have made. Ease out the belly a little more if the transition of the curve is not flowing as you imagine it should.

5. With the wheel turning at a medium to slow speed, use a throwing rib to remove the excess throwing slurry and form a slightly straighter wall area at the neck, which can then be used to ease out the throat of the jug.

WHEEL MEDIUM SLOW

WHEEL MEDIUM SPEED

STOP THE WHEEL

6. Compress the rim with a piece of chamois or thin polythene. Neaten the bottom edge with an angled cut and remove the water from the inside with a sponge. Cut through the base with a wire.

7. While the body is wet and on the wheelhead, use your forefinger and thumb to contain the sides of the jug while stroking out a lip with the wet forefinger of the other hand. Start by easing out the throat, moving from side to side.

8. Thin the edge of the lip in this way, too, to prevent the lip from dripping liquid. Create a channel in line with the throat and lip rim to direct the liquid into the centre of the lip. This will give the jug a good pouring action. Keep your finger wet while doing this.

9. Once the body has firmed to leather-hard, attach your handle (see pages 152 to 157). Score and slurry both attaching areas and wiggle the handle onto the scored body area to knit the surfaces together. Do this directly in line with the pouring lip.

10. Form a generous curve to the handle.

11. Angle-cut the bottom edge to your desired length before slurrying and scoring the two attaching areas. Press down this bottom end with a damp sponge to make a good join, and remove any excess slurry or score marks.

Leave the jug to dry slowly before biscuit-firing it to a temperature of 1,000ºC.

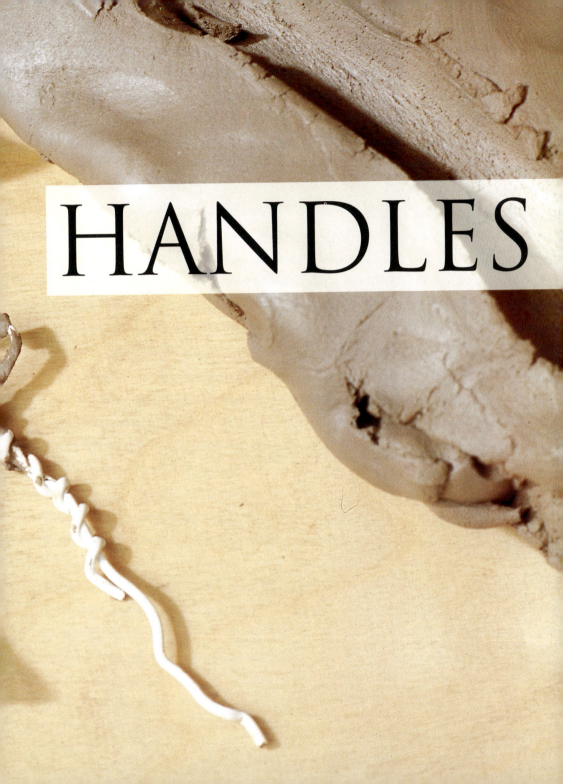

HANDLES

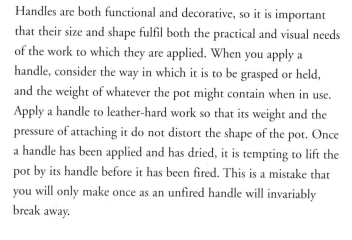

Handles are both functional and decorative, so it is important that their size and shape fulfil both the practical and visual needs of the work to which they are applied. When you apply a handle, consider the way in which it is to be grasped or held, and the weight of whatever the pot might contain when in use. Apply a handle to leather-hard work so that its weight and the pressure of attaching it do not distort the shape of the pot. Once a handle has been applied and has dried, it is tempting to lift the pot by its handle before it has been fired. This is a mistake that you will only make once as an unfired handle will invariably break away.

There are various methods of making handles: directly by hand, by a machine method called extrusion or from a mould. The examples in this section show how to make handles directly by hand. Dry any work that you make with a handle attachment slowly. This will give the pot and handle time to catch up with each other in terms of their moisture content, and will prevent the handle from cracking at the joining points due to a different shrinkage rate from that of the pot body. To slow down the drying time, carefully drape a piece of thin polythene over the pot and soft, joined handle, or leave the joined work somewhere not too warm and with little air circulation.

Once you have made a handle, apply it before it becomes too dry to bend (unless it is modelled), but while it is still firm enough to keep its shape. You can keep a handle at the correct consistency by wrapping it in thin polythene.

PULLING A HANDLE

The traditional method of forming handles is to 'pull' them from a lump of fairly stiff, well-prepared clay. A pulled handle fits the feel of a thrown pot because the clay is drawn out with water and pressure by hand, and the marks made are in keeping with the throwing rings of a wheel-made pot. The handle can be totally pulled before applying it to the work or partially pulled and continued from a stump that is attached to the pot.

Pulling from a lump of clay is done with a wet hand and requires the clay to be held at eye level so that you can see the profile shape as it is drawn out. It is best done over a bucket or sink, both to catch the drips and to enable you to wet your hand easily as you continue the task.

1. Start by squeezing the prepared lump of clay into an elongated shape at the end.

2. Wet your pulling hand and position it with your thumb towards you and your fingers flat behind it. The flat fingers act as a support as the flat area of your thumb does the work of exerting pressure on the clay. Starting at the top of the lump, drag down the clay with your fingers and flat thumb into a thick stump. Exert pressure evenly so as to keep the section of the stump even throughout. Continue to wet your working hand as you apply pressure to prevent any friction from tearing the stump.

4. When you have a strap that is even in section and to the length that you require, change the position of your hand to refine the shape. Keeping your fingers flat at the back as a support, run the tip of your thumb down the strap to create flat ridges that are in keeping with the surface quality of the pot to which you are going to apply it.

3. As you make each pulling stroke, change the position of your thumb as you draw out the clay to round the edges of the handle.

5. Lay the strap on a clean, wooden board or table and bring your finger down at the edge of the strap to break it to the required length.

CUTTING A HANDLE
FROM A BLOCK

This method of pulling a wire through a block of clay is a low-tech way of extruding a handle. Use a block of soft clay that has been well prepared to ensure that any air pockets have been removed. The wire hoop can be formed to make a handle section to suit your required size and shape.

1. Lay the prepared block of clay on a flat surface. Starting at the end of the block, pull the wire hoop towards you, while holding it level.

2. Carefully open up the block.

3. Lift out the handle and place it on a clean board or work surface.

CUTTING A HANDLE FROM A SHEET OF CLAY

1. Roll out a sheet of clay (see page 50, rolling out a slab) to the thickness that you require your handle to be. Use a ruler or any straight edge to cut a strip from the clay using a potter's knife. Gauge the width of your strip so that it is in keeping with the size of your pot.

2. Lift the strip onto a clean, wooden board or porous worktop and run a damp sponge along both outer edges. Turn the strip over and do the same on the other side. Compress the top of the strap with the sponge to prevent it from cracking when it is bent and joined into position. Trim your handle to the correct length as you position it in place.

MODELLING A HANDLE

1. Roughly shape a block of prepared clay into the shape and size that you require by holding up the shape to the body to which you are going to apply it and pinching out the shape with your fingers. Leave this shape to firm to leather-hard while wrapping the body of the pot in polythene to retain it at the leather-hard stage.

2. Use a potter's knife and a hacksaw blade to refine the shape and section of the handle.

3. Sponge the modelled handle to remove any unwanted tool marks. Trim the end of the handle to the correct length and shape as you position it in place.

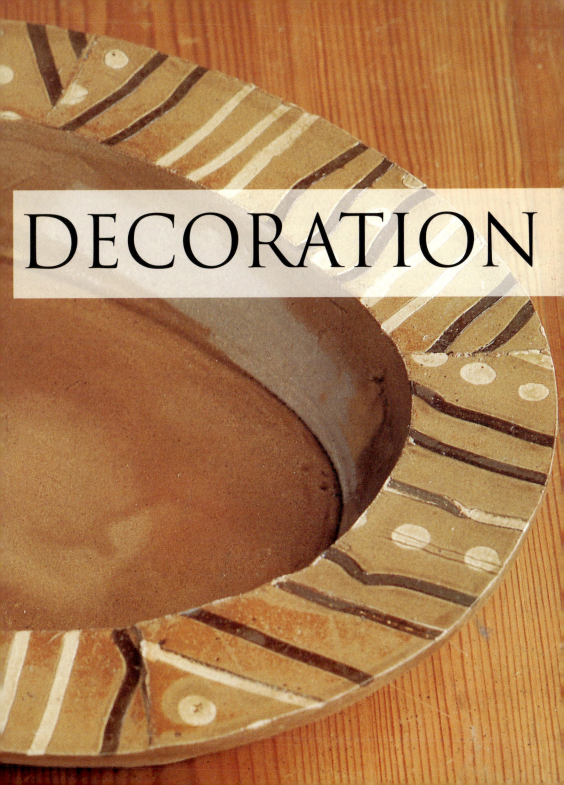

DECORATION

There are many different treatments that can be given to the clay surface, each with its own characteristic qualities. All of these methods are ancient, and can be seen in museum collections around the world. Each new generation of clay-makers claims them as its own by using them in a style that reflects its own time, subject matter, culture and interpretation.

This section is divided into two main areas. The first concentrates on methods of decoration into the clay, using the projects in the hand-building section to demonstrate them. The second concerns itself with techniques of slip-decorating, which are demonstrated on flat areas of clay. (The leather-hard-box project combines both clay- and slip-decorating methods.) Some of these slip-decorating techniques can be carried through to the biscuit stage, not with slip, but with other decorating materials, such as oxides and underglaze colours, stains and glaze.

It is worth remembering that techniques can be combined on the same piece of work (see the leather-hard-box project on page 170). For instance, it is possible to use resist slip-decorating methods on a surface that is textured or has raised sprigs. Thin slip can be applied over coloured clays to give a veiled appearance. The combinations are endless, and when different firing temperatures and glaze finishes are added to the equation, the possibilities increase still further. If you are a newcomer to clay, a step-by-step approach will build your understanding of each material and technique. It is, however, worth taking notes about how you came to a particular result so that you will be able to repeat (and improve) these processes and techniques in order to enhance your clay-work.

CLAY-DECORATING

Tools

1 **Clay gun and dies (1a).**
2 **Metal kidney.**
3 **Looped modelling tool.**
4 **Knife**
5 **Hacksaw blade and surform blade for carving.**
6 **Stamps.**
7 **Roulettes.**
8 **Textured materials.**
9 **Sprig moulds.**
10 **Sgraffito tool or pencil.**

The colour and texture of your clay will have an effect on your decoration and should be chosen with the final result in mind. A white or light clay will give a better colour response than a dark clay. If you want to lighten the background colour of a dark clay, a covering of white or light slip can be applied that will respond to colour in a similar way to a white or light clay. Sand or grog in a clay often reveals itself in the decoration by bleeding into a glaze at high stoneware temperatures. As a beginner, it is important to remember that clay cannot be applied to clay once it has become bone dry, or once it has gone through the firing process.

Roulettes and sprig moulds.

The following techniques illustrate methods of decorating using clay.

Clay-gun technique
The pinched-bottle project (continued from pages 69–72)

A clay gun extrudes soft clay in long strings. The profile shape of the extruded string is chosen from a selection of nozzles supplied with the gun. The extruded clay should be the same as the clay of the body of the work to which you are attaching the pieces, or else with a similar shrinkage rate.

1. When the bottle has firmed to leather-hard, extrude strings of the profiled shape using soft, prepared clay.

2. Cut the extruded pieces to the required length and apply them before they become too firm to bend without cracking. Slurry and score the area where each extrusion is to be attached.

3. Push each extruded piece onto the scored area with a damp sponge so as not to damage the shape or surface of the soft clay. Use a damp paintbrush to remove any excess slurry and score marks. Dry the bottle slowly so that the extruded pieces have a chance to even in moisture content to prevent them from cracking when being dried and fired.

Texture and stamping techniques
The hump-mould-bowl project (continued from pages 89–92)

Texture can be applied to soft clay in a number of ways, by pressing objects into the clay or by rolling textured materials onto the surface with a rolling pin. By applying the texture to a slab that is then placed face down onto a hump mould, the texture is not lost on the upper face of the bowl. The finishing-off work with tools is carried out on the outer face of the bowl. The texture can be picked up using slips at the leather-hard stage or ceramic underglaze colour or oxides at the biscuit-fired stage (see page 222 to find out how this is done).

Print the texture into the soft slab, pressing objects into the surface of the clay.

Alternatively, roll textured material, such as corrugated paper, raised wallpaper or mesh, into the clay.

Roulettes can also be used to stamp texture into the clay. You can either carve them from clay and biscuit-fire them or else buy them ready-made.

Raised clay sprigs
The relief-tile project (continued from pages 103–5)

Plaster sprig moulds (see page 103) produce raised pieces of clay that can be attached to the leather-hard surface of clay-work once they have firmed to leather-hard. Sprig moulds can be cast in plaster from found objects or from modelled clay. Objects pressed into clay, which is then biscuit-fired, also make workable sprig moulds. The clay that you use to make a sprig should be the same as that used for the work to which you are going to attach it, or with a similar shrinkage rate.

1. To take a pressing from a sprig mould, force soft clay down, into the hollow of your mould, with your fingers or a thumb.

2. Level off the clay using a flat tool, being careful not to scrape any plaster into the clay.

3. Lift out the sprig, using a small piece of wet clay to make a handle. Give the sprig a wiggle to help to loosen it from the sides of the mould.

4. Allow the sprig to firm to leather-hard before trimming up the edges or hollowing out the back if it is very thick (see step 8).

5. Attach it to the clay surface by slurrying and scoring both attaching surfaces.

6. Use a damp sponge to apply gentle pressure to knit the sprig into position without damaging its surface. Remove any excess slurry with a sponge or paintbrush before it dries.

7. You can carve back into a sprig while it is still leather-hard to add pieces that butt up to its edges.

8. If your sprig is very thick, hollow it out when it is leather-hard, using a looped-wire modelling tool, before attaching it.

Carving
The coiling project (continued from pages 73–77)

Carving into clay to achieve a sharp, crisp finish is best done
when the clay is leather-hard. Large areas of clay can be removed
with a looped modelling tool, a knife or a surform blade. Finer
areas can be pared away using a piece of hacksaw blade. The
marks made by the tools can be smoothed away with a damp
sponge or can be left to give a vigorous, worked surface.

Use a hacksaw blade to pare
contours in the clay.

Use a knife or hooped-wire tool
to carve into the surface of
the clay.

Use a hacksaw blade to carve the
clay finely.

CLAY- AND SLIP-DECORATING

Inlaid clay

The soft-slab-dish project (continued from pages 78–82)

This technique uses different-coloured clays with a similar shrinkage rate. The coloured clays are arranged on soft sheets of clay and rolled into its surface. These sheets are then cut and used to make the soft-slab dish. You can also use coloured clays for this technique. If you want to know how to make colour additions to a light- or white-coloured clay, see page 99.

1. First of all, arrange your prepared, soft clays of differing colours.

2. Keep your rolling pin clean for this technique, or else use a piece of clean newspaper on the surface of the clay to prevent one colour of clay from contaminating another.

3. Roll the coloured clays into the backing sheet of clay with a rolling pin while the clay is still soft. You can use rolling slats as a guide to keep the section even.

4. Peel back the paper.

5. Allow the clay to firm to leather-hard before cutting it into useable strips to complete the dish. Once the clay dish has firmed to the dry side of leather-hard, the surface of the coloured clays can be scraped back with a metal kidney to reveal the defined areas of the different-coloured clays.

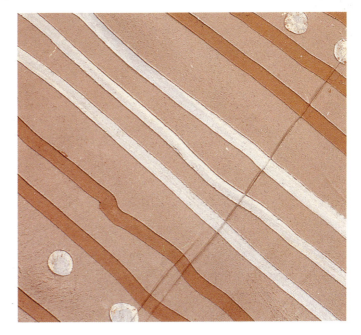

Paper resist, wax resist and sgraffito
The leather-hard-slab-box project
(continued from pages 83–88)

To decorate the leather-hard-slab box, a combination of three decorating techniques is used on top of a brushed-slip ground. Paper-resist shapes are first laid down on top of the first, ground, layer of white slip. Next, another layer of white slip is laid down around the paper shapes. Wax-resist solution is then painted over the second layer of slip, which is scratched through to the surface of the clay. These lines are then filled with underglaze colour.

1.   Apply a layer of slip with a wide, soft brush to the surface of the box and allow it to become touch-dry again.

2.   When the slip is touch-dry, place cut pieces of newsprint paper down on it to create an overall pattern.

3.   Now sponge their edges down, into place, using a damp sponge.

4. Apply a second layer of white slip with the soft, wide brush.

5. When the second layer of slip is touch-dry, paint the surface of the box with a layer of wax-resist solution and allow it to dry completely. It is not necessary to paint over the paper as this acts as a resist layer, too.

6. Scratch lines through the wax into the surface of the leather-hard clay with a sgraffito tool or pencil.

7. Fill the lines with a thin wash of underglaze colour. This will give an etched feel to the drawn lines.

8. Peel away the paper before leaving the box to dry for biscuit-firing. The slip will have a veil-like quality where the paper shapes were placed because there is only one layer of slip here.

METHODS OF APPLYING SLIPS, COLOUR AND GLAZE

Slip is a smooth, liquid coating of clay that is applied to the surface of clay-work to give colour, and often to create a design or a contrasting colour or surface texture to the clay. Slips are made from clay and water, but other ingredients are often added to give colour and to adjust the slip to fit the clay body as it shrinks in the drying and firing processes. Decorating slips are not the same as the slurry that is used to join clay-work together, nor are they the same as the clay-casting slips used for pouring into plaster moulds to create clay-work forms. The higher the temperature of the final glaze firing, the greater the interaction between the slip and glaze as the two fuse and react together in the kiln. The finished result will depend on which glaze you chose to place over the top of the slip at the biscuit-fired stage.

Another term that is sometimes used for slip is 'engobe'. Both slips and engobes can be applied at the leather-hard stage. But an engobe can also be applied at the biscuit-fired stage. An engobe also differs from a slip in that although it is technically a liquid clay, it is really halfway between a slip and a glaze because it contains a fluxing material. This fluxing material melts the engobe sufficiently to give it a smoother final finish than a slip, removing the necessity for a glaze application and firing.

Commercial slip recipes

Commercially prepared decorating slips can be bought from ceramic suppliers in powdered or slop form ready for soaking and/or sieving. It is possible to buy a white slip and to stain it using colouring oxides or stains to make up a range of different colours for decorating purposes (see page 195). Any slip, whether it is bought in powdered or slop form, will require sieving through a 60- to 80-mesh sieve to give it an even consistency throughout.

Sieving

Sieving slip combines the ingredients to a smooth consistency. A sieve's mesh number denotes how many holes are present per square inch. The higher the number, the finer the mesh of the sieve and the slower the sieving will be. Small test sieves are used for smaller quantities of sieving, and larger sieves for bucket-sized batches. Do not try to push a powdered slip through a sieve – add the water first and mix it thoroughly before passing it through the sieve as shown in the photo below. Remember to wear a dust mask when you are handling powdered materials.

Sieve the wet ingredients at least two or three times, supporting the sieve with slats on the rim of a bucket. Push the wet ingredients through with a sieve or washing-up brush. You can use a rubber kidney to clean the ingredients off the sides of the bucket and to help push stubborn lumps through the mesh of the sieve.

Consistency

Once you have sieved the slip, check its consistency by stirring it and then dipping in a dry finger and looking at the coverage. The correct consistency will vary according to the technique that you use. If a mix is too thick, add water a little at a time until it feels right. If it is too thin, it will have to be left overnight to settle, after which water can be pulled, poured or scooped off the top. The slip can then be taken back to the required consistency by stirring in a little water at a time.

If you are applying slip to decorate your work, your work must be leather-hard. Do not try to pick up your work once you have applied the decoration until it has also dried to leather-hard. It is advisable to position your work on a board so that you can move it once it has been decorated or until it is firm enough to take a second layer of decoration. Decorating equipment and any spillage of slip colour and glaze should be cleaned directly with a wet sponge to keep the dust levels down.

SLIP-DECORATING

Tools

1 **Scissors:** for cutting newsprint paper for paper resist.

2 **Newsprint paper:** for paper resist.

3 **Wax resist:** to repel areas of slip.

4 **Latex resist:** to create a barrier to applied colour.

5 **Paintbrushes:** soft, flat brushes are best for applying slip.

6 **Slip-trailer:** for laying down fluid lines of slip.

7 **Sponge:** for applying slip.

8 **Sgraffito tool or pencil:** for scratching through slip.

9 **Metal kidney:** for scraping back slip.

Painting and pouring slip

Poured slip that is the consistency of single cream gives a solid coverage to leather-hard clay. When slip is poured over the entire surface of a piece of work, the clay wall absorbs the moisture in the slip and expands, which can sometimes cause a rim or wall to split. To minimise this risk, make sure that the clay onto which you are pouring the slip is at the firm end of the scale of leather-hardness, and that the walls of the work are even in section.

Pour any internal faces of slip before the external face of a pot. The internal slip must be left to become leather-hard before applying any slip to the outside wall of your piece of work.

Painted slip will give a more broken, or veil-type, coverage to the clay unless you apply two or three layers. Paint on the slip at milk consistency and build up layers if you require an overall, flat coverage. Two to three thin layers of slip will give flatter coverage than one thick layer of slip. Brushstrokes using slips or any ceramic colour, such as oxides or underglaze, are exaggerated when subsequently covered by a transparent glaze and fired. Choose the right brush for the result that you want to achieve. To apply slip to a large surface area, use a wide, flat, soft brush.

Paper resist (see page 170, the leather-hard-slab-box project)

Paper resist gives a hard, clean edge that can be picked up at a later stage with a wash of colour or that can be combined with other methods of decoration. (Masking tape on biscuit-fired ware can be used to resist glaze when decorating.)

1. Use a non-shiny paper, such as newspaper, to cut out the shapes that you are going to use for your design. Quickly pass the cut shapes through water to dampen them and then apply them to the leather-hard clay surface. Press their edges down with your fingertips or a sponge to make sure that they are positioned firmly in place and that they are flat, so that no slip can seep underneath them.

2. Apply the slip with a soft, flat brush, using strokes that move away from the edges of the shapes.

3. Once the slip is touch-dry, peel the paper away. You can go on to add subsequent layers of slip by realigning paper shapes over the first layer. Doing this will create some interesting effects.

Wax resist (see page 170, the leather-hard-slab-box project)

Wax-resist solution creates a characteristically soft, broken edge, dotted with random droplets of colour. Once applied, wax resist can only be removed by burning it out in the firing process. You can also use wax resist to repel areas of glaze at the biscuit-fired stage. To prevent dry wax resist from spoiling your brush, rinse it or immerse it in water as soon as you have finished painting.

1. The wax must be completely dry before any slip is applied. Thin the slip to a milky consistency to make sure that the dry wax repels the slip.

2. Lines scratched through the dried wax can be painted over with colour to give the appearance of an etched line, which makes a good contrast to the mottled wax-resist effect.

Latex resist

Latex-resist solution can be peeled off once it has dried. It leaves a sharper edge and a clean finish and can be used to block out tight, graphic or fluid, painterly shapes. Because it peels off, subsequent layers of slip or colour can be applied over the first latex-resist area. To prevent latex-resist solution from spoiling your brush, rinse it or immerse it in water as soon as you have finished painting.

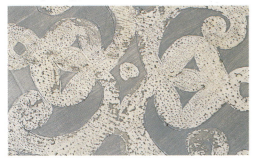 

1. The latex resist must be completely dry before applying the slip, which can be of any consistency.

2. Allow the slip to become touch-dry before peeling the latex away.

Sponging

A sponge can be used to apply slip to create a dappled effect. Or you can print designs by cutting shapes from a flat sponge. This technique requires the slip to be of a milk-to-single-cream consistency. This method of sponging can also be used to apply ceramic colour, oxides or glaze at the biscuit-fired stage.

Pick up the slip or colour with the sponge, without overly saturating it or causing it to drip. Sponged slip can be applied either directly to the clay surface or over a layer of constrasting-coloured slip that is touch-dry.

Slip-trailing

Slip-trailers are traditional decorating tools that are used to trail raised lines or dots of slip. The slip for this technique should be of a thin-yoghurt consistency. Clean out the trailer by returning any unused slip to its container and rinsing the trailer through with clean water before the slip dries inside the trailer. You can also use this technique to apply glaze to biscuitware.

Fill the slip-trailer by squeezing out the air in the bulb by holding the tip under the slip and then letting go of the bulb to pull the slip in. Press the bulb gently and move the trailer along swiftly as the slip comes out of the nozzle. This technique looks easy, but it's hard to achieve a smooth action on a curve. This requires a lot of practice!

Sgraffito (see page 170, the leather-hard-slab-box project)

Sgraffito is an Italian term meaning 'to scratch'. Slip is first applied to the clay surface and allowed to firm to leather-hard. By scratching away areas of slip, or by drawing lines through the slip, the underlying colour of the clay is revealed to give some contrast to the design. This technique can also be used to scratch through glaze on biscuit-fired ware.

Wait until the slip is firm enough to fall away from the surface of the clay without creating a burr that sticks to the surface. Use a pointed tool or a pencil to make a line through the slip. Areas of slip can also be scratched away using a sharp-edged, looped-wire tool. Brush away the removed slip to ensure that the scratched areas are smooth once they are fired.

Washing back or inlay

Slip can be painted into texture or sgraffito lines and can then be wiped or scraped back to highlight the textured or lined surface. This technique can also be used to highlight areas of texture using glaze or underglaze colour at the biscuit-fired stage.

This technique works best if the textured area is quite deep. Push the slip down, into the crevices of the textured surface, with a loaded paintbrush. Wait for the slip and clay to firm again to leather-hard before scraping back the surface slip on the high areas of the textured clay. You will achieve a cleaner finish if the clay and slip are on the firm-to-dry side of leather-hard.

Dry brush

The converse of the inlay method to highlight texture is to use a partially loaded, soft, flat paintbrush to give a contrasting colour to the protruding areas. Again, this technique can be used not only at the leather-hard stage using slips, but also at the biscuit-fired stage using oxides and underglaze colours, as well as glaze.

Load your paintbrush with slip, then scrape back some of its content on the sharp edge of the container. Rapidly move your brush in sweeping strokes, loading it with just enough slip to paint the high areas of texture, without allowing any slip to run down, into the sunken areas of clay.

OXIDES AND COLOUR

Oyster square by Christine Hester Smith.

2 Tall Jugs. Height 35 and 33cm.
Karen Bunting.

Clay-workers develop a particular feel for their work, and colour choice is an important aspect of this. The possibilities and permutations using ceramic colour are endless. Many colour additions to a base glaze or slip can also have an effect on the texture of the finished, fired and glazed work. Add to this the fact that combinations of these additions have an interactive and sometimes unexpected effect, and the area of 'tinkering with glaze' becomes very exciting. The best way to approach the slip, glaze and colour area is by means of methodical experimentation. However, a word of warning! There is nothing more frustrating than finally attaining a result for which you have long been searching only to find that you have forgotten to jot a particular test or ingredient into your notebook.

Like painting on canvas or paper, there is no right or wrong way in which ceramic colour should be applied. What you choose to paint, draw, trail, pour or sponge into place is both personal and revealing. As a beginner, it is helpful to keep a record of consistencies and strengths, and when and where you applied materials, to build your knowledge of what works and what doesn't. In this way, you will begin to build a personal repertoire of colour particular to your own style and work. Decorating techniques using colour are executed at different stages of the clay-work – leather-hard, dry, biscuit-fired or glaze-fired. The colouring materials that you use will decide whether decoration is to happen at just one of these stages or at a combination of stages.

Tools and materials

1 **Brushes:** select your brush according to the effect that you want to achieve and/or the technique that you are using.

2 **Gum arabic:** mixed with warm water, this will enable powdered colour to adhere to your work without it rubbing off while you handle the work for glazing.

3 **Oxides:** the colour range is available in many forms, powder (4), liquid (5), tube (6), crayon (7) and pan (8).

In this book, the colour range includes colouring oxides, underglaze colours and stains. Ceramic colour is derived from naturally occurring materials mined from the earth's surface. These naturally occurring colouring oxides can be used on their own to decorate your work, or they can be used in conjunction with underglaze colours and stains, which are a controlled blend of colouring oxides combined with stabilising material.

The naturally occurring oxides, painted under a transparent glaze, fired to 1,060°C (earthenware temperature). Each of these oxides imparts a particular colour characteristic to a universal ceramic palette.

Different oxides and their uses

Most of the metallic oxides are mined in the form of ores that are smelted and ground. The oxides used for ceramic colour are sometimes found in varying forms, such as cobalt, which is used as a carbonate, as well as in oxide form. The carbonate is chosen to colour a glaze blue when a less grainy or speckled effect is sought. Some oxides are heavier or coarser than others, while others will disperse more readily.

With exceptions, such as copper, all of the oxides are stable at low temperatures, while at higher temperatures, some become volatile and can affect neighbouring work in the kiln.

The most commonly used oxides for ceramic work are iron, manganese, copper, cobalt, chrome, rutile, vanadium, nickel and ilmenite. In dark or red clays, iron oxide is present, and the colour in these clays reacts with the glaze when the work is fired to high temperatures in the stoneware range. This interaction of oxide and glaze can give pleasing results, such as breaks in the glaze at high or textured parts of the clay surface. Equally, colouring oxides applied to light clay as decoration or in slips do the same by reacting with the glaze at high temperatures. When colouring oxides are applied under a glaze on their own, or when contained in decorating slips at low temperatures in the earthenware range, there is little, or less, of this interaction with the glaze. When oxides are used to colour a glaze, the ingredients in the glaze recipe will affect the colour produced by that oxide.

Oxides used in a glaze

The confusing aspect of ceramic oxides is that the powders are a completely different colour from their fired results. It is therefore important to label their containers well!

Cobalt oxide or carbonate. Cobalt is usually used as cobalt carbonate in glazes because of its fine particle size. Black cobalt oxide is a black powder. Cobalt is a strong and reliable oxide, giving vivid colour in alkaline glazes, deeper blues in lead glazes and good colour variations when used in combination with other oxides.

Copper oxide or carbonate. Copper is commonly used as copper carbonate because it has finer particles. Copper gives greens when oxidised, turquoise blues in alkaline glazes, bottle greens in lead glazes, intense blue-greens in barium glazes and reds in high-fired, reduction glazes. It is volatile when fired above 1,250°C (which means that it will disappear in the firing).

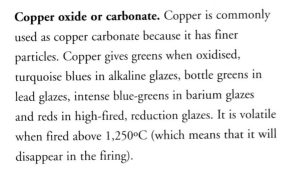

Chromium oxide. Chrome oxide gives a rather flat, lifeless colour when it is used on its own as a painted oxide. It can, however, give orange to red in low-fired lead glazes, brown when used with zinc and pink in tin glazes with small additions of 1 per cent. It is volatile above 1,200°C in tin glazes.

Red and black iron oxide. Red iron oxide has finer particles than black iron oxide or crocus martis, which are used to give a speckled effect in high-fired or stoneware glazes. Iron oxide gives bright amber tones in lead glazes when used at 2–5 per cent. It gives cream to red-brown colours in lead or tin glazes and yellow to tan colours in alkaline glazes.

Manganese oxide. Added as manganese carbonate (a pink powder), or as the finer-particled manganese dioxide, it gives a rich blue-plum colour in high-alkaline glazes. In lead glazes, manganese gives a softer-purple colour tinge with brown. Combined with small amounts of cobalt, it can also give a rich violet colour.

Nickel oxide. Nickel is added as a green or black nickel-oxide powder. It works best in combination with other oxides to give a subtle grey hue to other colours, such as cobalt or iron oxide.

Vanadium pentoxide. Vanadium pentoxide is usually used as a stain in glazes in combination with tin oxide to give an opaque glaze.

Rutile. Rutile is used as an ore containing titanium and iron oxide. It gives a weak tint and is more commonly used to give dramatic texture to a glaze of broken or mottled colour, although it does not have this effect in lead glazes. With other oxides, i.e., iron, cobalt, copper and chrome, rutile gives pleasingly hued and textured colours. Rutile is also widely used in crystalline glazes.

Ilmenite. Ilmenite is used to give a granular or spotty effect, or else to give texture, to a glaze. The ore contains titanium and iron oxide.

Painting oxides under a glaze

If you want to give bright colours to fired work when painting oxides beneath a glaze or under glaze colours, then a light-bodied clay should be chosen, or a white or light slip background should be used to cover a dark or red clay. The work should then be applied with a transparent glaze at the biscuit-fired stage and fired to a low earthenware temperature. This lower temperature enables such colours as bright reds and yellows to be achieved more easily (these are often the first colours to be lost in the higher temperature range of stoneware).

Maiolica or inglaze

The term 'colour', when used in connection with ceramic decoration, describes the use of body stains, underglazes and colouring oxides that can be applied to leather-hard, dry and biscuit-fired clay, both under and over the powdered-glazed surface. When colouring oxides are applied on top of the dry, powdery, unfired (often white) glaze before the work is placed in the kiln for the final glaze-firing, it is often given the descriptive name 'maiolica' or 'inglaze'. This method of inglaze decoration can be used on any glaze, not just a white one. It allows the colour to sink into the glaze surface at higher temperatures, and often gives a diffused quality to the fired colour.

Light coloured clay was used for these bottles-essential when trying to achieve bright colours.

Onglaze or enamel colours

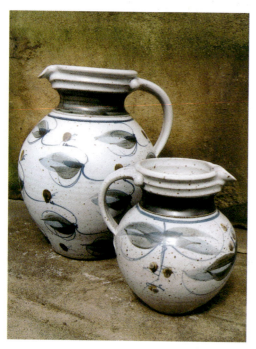

Andrew Hague's large, fat jugs. Talc glaze with onglaze brushwork was used for these.

There is also a further opportunity to apply colour to fired work, i.e., on top of the fired-glaze surface with strongly coloured, low-temperature glazes. These colours are called 'onglaze' and often go under the name of 'enamels' or 'overglaze'. Onglaze colours are fired to a lower temperature than glaze (see page 249), and are applied to the hard-fired-glaze surface (which should be shiny). This is why the technique is often referred to as china-painting. Onglaze colours can be bought in oil- and water-based forms. The traditional, powdered-enamel colours are often laid on using various types of oil-based mediums. This book does not go into detail about china-painting and the way that colours are mixed using such mediums, but water-based enamels are straightforward to use.

In the glaze section, the opportunity to stain white and transparent glazes is discussed as a method of applying colour to the biscuit-fired work (see page 194).

*Blue bottles with an alkaline, earthenware glaze stained
with a 5 per cent cobalt-oxide addition to the base
transparent glaze, which fires to 1,060°C. This glaze was
chosen to pick out the raised clay decoration.*

Colouring oxides

Naturally occurring metallic oxides give the characteristic hues seen on all historic ceramic work, and have a soft, textural quality that is distinctively different to flatter, commercial underglaze and stain colours. They come in a powdered form, which can be intermixed or used singly. Oxides can be used for staining light-bodied clays and for staining slips or glazes. Oxides can also be used as painted colour on their own by mixing the powdered oxide with water to approximately watercolour consistency. Some of the oxides, such as copper carbonate, have a tendency to settle quickly and should be stirred before loading the brush. Their use and strength of application is learnt from the fired result, as each oxide differs. Oxides used neat for colour application onto biscuit-fired work can be suspended in gum arabic to enable them to adhere to the clay surface so that they do not fall into the glaze when you are applying glaze over decoration. There are also mediums available to suspend powdered colour for such tasks as screen-printing or onglaze decorating.

Oxides are deceiving in powdered form as their true, finished colour is nowhere near how they appear in their raw, powdered state. For example, cobalt in the carbonate form is a pink powder, and in the oxide form, it is black. Either one of these will give a strong blue when it interacts with fired glaze. Because of this, when it comes to decorating, it is difficult to 'see what you are doing' until the kiln door is opened after the final glaze-firing!

Underglaze colours and stains

Underglaze colours and stains are commercially produced, intermixable colours made up of a controlled blend of colour oxides and stabilising materials. They are available in a huge colour range. Underglaze colours and stains can be used for all of the same purposes as colouring oxides. They are obtainable from suppliers in a number of forms, and with differing brand names. The colours are 'flatter' or 'harsher' than naturally occurring metallic oxides, and are often used as a means of obtaining reds or yellows that are difficult to achieve with oxides. Underglaze colours and stains have the advantage of colour stability and are a quickly obtainable means of achieving differing hues of the same colour. Suppliers indicate what temperature the underglaze colours and stains can be fired to before the colour disappears, but ignoring this advice can sometimes result in unexpected and pleasing results. Underglaze colours and stains can be intermixed and used alongside colouring oxides. Underglazes and stains in liquid form contain a carrying medium, binder and flux that are not always suitable for staining a glaze.

Adding ceramic colour to commercial recipes

All of the decorative processes explained in this book can be utilised for coloured glazes, including brushing.

Commercially prepared slips and glazes can be bought from ceramic suppliers in powdered form ready for soaking and sieving. Choose your glaze to fit the firing range of the clay body that you are using and its final firing temperature. Colours and finished textures of a glaze can be selected from a supplier's catalogue in the same way as selecting paint from a colour chart. A base transparent or white glaze can be coloured in differing proportions as a method of decorating biscuit-fired work. All of the decorative processes described in the slip-decorating section, including brushing, sponging, trailing, scraping, wax resist and sgraffito, can be used when decorating with coloured glazes. Paper-resist decoration should be adapted by using masking tape on the biscuit clay when using coloured glaze on a biscuit-clay surface. Applying an overall covering of glaze (see page 213) can be thought of as a decorative process in itself. The colour and texture of glaze can in itself enhance a form or surface area.

Additions of colour to a base glaze or slip using colouring oxides, underglazes and body stains

Commercial and made-up white or transparent glazes and white slips can be used as a base and varied by making measured colour additions using stains or oxides while in their dry state. The colouring additions for slips and glazes altered in this way should be test-fired before use on finished work. To test a glaze, a vertical tile or the inside of a small bowl is preferable to a horizontal test tile to give a good indication of the fluidity of the glaze. If the glaze runs down the test piece, it is going to do the same on finished work, and could cause the work to become bonded to the kiln shelf with cooled molten glaze. (It is wise to assume that when making colour additions to a glaze, the glaze from any test piece is likely to drip or flow onto whatever the piece is sitting on in the kiln.)

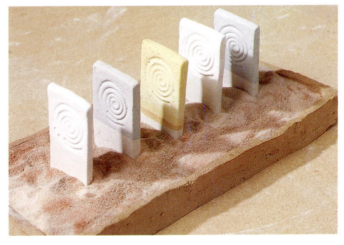

To protect kiln shelves from glaze drips, stand your test pieces on a purpose-made tray constructed from a sheet of clay, with a low wall attached to its edge. Layer the tray with silica sand to prevent any test pieces from sticking to the tray.

Colour additions need to be weighed before adding water and sieving them because they are added to the base glaze or slip as a percentage of dry weight. To weigh small amounts of colour additions, accurate scales showing suitable fractions of a gram are a necessary piece of equipment (see page 196).

Tools

1   **Scales:** there are many types of weighing equipment available, ranging from accurate digital scales to various balancing scales with separate weights. Most scales will give a sufficiently accurate reading for bulk weights, but a fine scale is necessary for smaller amounts, such as oxide additions to glazes, and for weighing out small quantities of glaze, slip and colour additions for testing.

2   **Sieve, test sieve and brush:** sieves vary in mesh size from 20 to 200# (holes per 2.5cm² or square inch). The optimum for sieving ceramic colour, glaze and slip is 60–80#. Test sieves are more appropriate when dealing with small quantities of ingredients.

3   **Plastic cups and indelible pen:** glazes look very similar when in slop form, so label containers like plastic cups with an indelible pen.

4   **Health and safety equipment, apron, mask, surgical gloves, large cleaning sponge:** precautions should be taken when preparing dry materials to avoid inhaling particles of airborne dust. A mask that meets the appropriate particle-size safety standards (BS60 16 TYPE 2) should be worn when handling any powdered ceramic materials.

Simple testing for colour additions to a base glaze or slip

When making up a glaze or slip from a dry, powder form, you will need a container at least twice the size of the volume that you are mixing to allow the addition of approximately 100ml of water to every 100g of materials. Allow the water to soak in thoroughly before mixing and sieving the base glaze or slip with your colour additions. As you tip in each addition, mark the container with an indelible pen to record what you have added.

To test additions to a base slip or glaze, weigh out 100g quantities of the powder base into plastic containers. This amount fits comfortably into an empty plastic drinking cup. Weigh each colour addition as a percentage of the 100g in its powdered form. For example, 0.5 per cent of 100g will be 0.5g of cobalt tipped into 100g of base slip or glaze. If you wanted to repeat this colour test for a larger quantity of slip or glaze, then for this example, every 1kg of slip or glaze would need 5g of colour to achieve the same result as the test.

Make up a number of tests, varying the percentages of the colouring oxide, oxide combinations, underglaze or body stain. When the fired result emerges from the glaze-firing, you will find out the correct percentage addition of colour required to achieve the colour that you require.

By looking at the list of the percentage additions of each oxide shown on page 198, you will be able to start to gauge the strengths of each of the oxides, as well as the type of colour result that you can achieve. The strength of every oxide varies because each has its own individual properties. The percentage information given also indicates what can be expected when oxides are combined with water when decorating with neat colouring oxides. You will see that such oxides as cobalt need very little to make a strong colour blue, and the same is true when you paint neat cobalt oxide and water directly onto the clay with a brush. The type of glaze and its fired temperature will also affect the final result. Another factor that will affect your final fired-glaze result is the colour of the clay to which you apply the glaze.

The interaction of clay and colour is more pronounced at the higher, or stoneware, temperature range. As a beginner, bear in mind that if you place a coloured slip under a glaze, it has the same effect as altering the colour of the clay because what you are doing when applying a slip is putting a veneer of differing-coloured clay under the glaze surface. Consider the fact that coloured decorating slips contain colouring oxides, and that by decorating one area of the clay surface and applying a coloured glaze over the top of that slip, a colour and/or textural contrast can be achieved to enhance your finished, fired work.

Copper oxide: 0.75% light turquoise, 1.5% mid-turquoise, 3% strong turquoise.

Cobalt oxide: 0.25% light navy blue, 0.5% mid-navy blue, 1% strong navy blue.

Red iron oxide: 3% cream, 6% honey, 12% dark honey.

Manganese dioxide: 1% light purple-brown, 2% mid-purple-brown, 4% dark purple-brown.

Chrome oxide: 0.25% light yellow-green, 0.5% mid-yellow-green, 1% strong yellow-green.

Rutile: 5% cream, 10% light beige, 15% beige-brown.

Vanadium pentoxide: 3% cream, 6% yellow-cream, 10% opaque cream-white.

Nickel oxide: 0.5% pale coffee-brown, 1% mid-coffee-brown, 2% dark coffee-brown.

Ilmenite: 3% cream, 6% mid-rust, 10% strong rust.

The glaze-test results above indicate the type of colour and strength that you will achieve if you make varying colour additions to any commercially bought transparent, alkaline, glaze that fires to 1,060°C when it is applied to a white clay.

If you add these same colour-percentage additions to a lead glaze that is fired to 1,060°C on white clay, the result will sometimes be strikingly different – particularly with copper oxide.

Copper oxide: light bottle-green, mid-bottle-green, dark copper-green, and less crazed.

Cobalt oxide: similar colour results, but less crazed.

Red iron oxide: light rust-brown, mid-rust-brown, dark coffee-brown.

Manganese dioxide: light coffee-brown, mid-coffee-brown, dark coffee-brown.

Chrome oxide: light, warm yellow, mid-warm yellow-brown, warm yellow-brown.

Rutile: light pinky-brown, mid-pinky-brown, dark pinky-brown.

Vanadium pentoxide: light yellow-cream, pitted yellow cream, yellow cream that crawls.

Nickel: light teddy-bear-brown, mid-teddy-bear-brown, dark teddy-bear-brown with green tinges.

Ilmenite: light honey, mid-honey, dark honey.

You can mark each test piece using iron oxide mixed with water. After you have tipped each ingredient into each cup and have marked them all clearly, cover the dry materials with water and allow the water to soak in. Mix the ingredients thoroughly by sieving each test three times. Pass the mixed, wet ingredients through the test sieve, pushing any stubborn particles through with a stiff paintbrush. If you start with the lower addition of colour for each oxide, the sieve and brush will only have to be cleaned once for each set of colour additions, instead of every time for each colour test. Make sure that you return the ingredients to the correctly marked cup, otherwise all of your hard work of weighing and sieving will go to waste!

Dipping to the correct consistency

If you are testing slips, you will need leather-hard test pieces (unless the slip is an engobe). If you are testing glazes, you will need biscuit-fired test pieces. Before dipping each test piece, stir the ingredients of each test. You can pour off the surplus water first to ensure that the sieved material is the correct consistency before you begin to stir. If it is too thick, you can add a little water, but you can't take the water out once the mixture has been stirred. Stir the ingredients well as colouring-oxide particles are heavy and will often sink to the bottom of a mix. Doing this will ensure that you have a true result of the tested mixed material. The correct consistency to dip a slip is like that of single cream, but a transparent glaze should be of skimmed-milk consistency. Other glazes, which are not transparent, should also be of single-cream consistency. Test the consistency by dipping a dry finger into the mix and looking at its coverage. Dip the test pieces into each mixture, holding them in for a count of two to three seconds. Leave a blank space of clay where you can record information on each test piece.

Making your test pieces

As you dip each test piece, mark it according to the test dipped. You can scratch through a leather-hard test piece with a pencil to do this. To mark a biscuit-fired test piece, use a fine paintbrush and a strong, watercolour-consistency solution of iron oxide mixed with water. It is helpful to record the final temperature at which it is fired. A code letter that corresponds to your notebook and marked cups is a quick method for marking each test. If you are testing a slip, your marking and recording in your notebook and on each test should be repeated at the glaze-application stage as you will also need to record what glaze you have used to cover the slip and the temperature at which it is fired.

Cross-blending tests

Once you have single-dipped each of the separate tests, you could try mixing equal proportions of each of the prepared tests and testing the colours when they are mixed together. This process, called 'cross-blending', will give an even wider range of subtle colour results.

The best glazes can often result from combining two or three colouring oxides. When mixing a spoonful of each glaze before applying them to the test piece, the percentages of the resulting mix are *halved* when they are combined. To give an accurate fired result, the glazes should be of the same water content, i.e., mixing tests 3+6, shown in example A, will become 2% vanadium pentoxide, 3% rutile, 4% etc. Keep the glazes in the top row with the same water content.

Example A

1. Iron, 4%. | 2. Copper, 2% & cobalt, 0.5%. | 3. Vanadium pentoxide, 6%.

4. Manganese, 6%. | 5. Nickel, 2%. | 6. Rutile, 8%.

1+2 1+3 1+4 1+5 1+6

2+3 2+4 2+5 2+6

3+4 3+5 3+6

4+5 4+6

5+6   *Cross-blending.*

Particularly exciting results can be achieved by cross-blending in the high temperature range. During such firings of around 1,280°C, the increased time and heat inside the kiln chamber can cause speckling and crystallisation to occur with particular base glazes.

The list of oxide combinations below shows the expected results when added to a glaze in the following percentage amounts. Similarly, slips can receive the same cross-blend treatment.

Oxide combinations	Expected colour result
Cobalt oxide, 0.5%, mixed with 2% iron oxide	Grey-blue
Cobalt, 0.5%, mixed with 5% manganese oxide	Purple-blue
Cobalt, 0.5%, mixed with 2% copper	Blue-green
Copper, 2%, mixed with 2% iron oxide	Warm green
Copper oxide, 3%, mixed with 3% vanadium	Yellow-green
Cobalt carbonate, 0.5%, mixed with 3% rutile	Warm blue
Vanadium, 5%, mixed with 4% rutile	Warm ochre

When using stains or underglaze colours to colour a base glaze or a slip, a percentage addition of approximately 10 per cent will give a strong colour result. The stabilising material used as an ingredient when using commercial stain and underglaze colour will usually result in a transparent glaze becoming opaque. To find out about the effect that the kiln-firing has on a glaze, and the different characteristics of various base glazes, see pages 206 to 207.

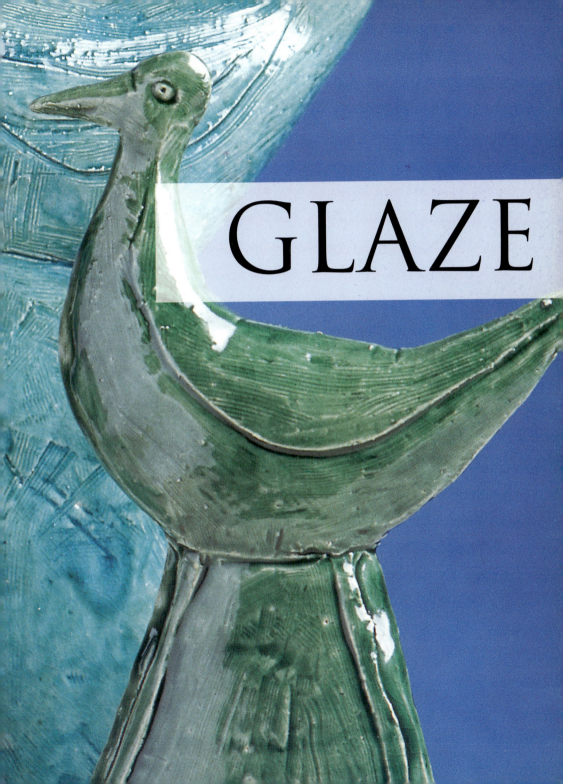

GLAZE

Many ceramic materials are toxic and should be handled with care. Powders should not be inhaled or ingested. When preparing glazes or slips, a mask should be worn and, in some cases, gloves, to prevent toxins (soda compounds) from being absorbed through the skin. A mask that conforms with safety standards should be worn when weighing glaze and colour. Working areas should be kept clean and free of glaze. Floors should preferably be washed down with water. Wear protective clothing and wash it regularly. Store materials in labelled, lidded containers. Keep ceramic materials away from children and pets.

Materials that should be treated with care include: aluminium-oxide sources, feldspars, clay, silica sources, quartz, flint, frits, sodium-oxide sources, soda feldspar, pearl ash, nitre, calcium-oxide sources, whiting, dolomite, lithium-oxide sources, spodumene, lepidolite, boron sources, borax, boric acid, magnesium-oxide sources, magnestite, talc, zinc, antimony, strontium, barium and most colouring oxides, stains and underglazes.

Lead

Some low-fired lead glazes are hazardous and should not be used in combination with copper or chromium oxide. These combinations are not suitable for the internal areas of domestic ware. Lead compounds, such as white or red lead, should be handled with great care, and fritted lead should be used as a matter of preference at all times (see frits, page 208).

GLAZE

Glaze is basically a layer of glass or silicate that is fused to a clay body by the heat of the kiln. Glaze is made up of three different elements: firstly, glass-forming materials, which make up a large part of the glaze; secondly, fluxes, which cause the glaze to melt or become fluid at specific temperatures; and, thirdly, stabilisers, such as aluminium oxide, which prevent the glaze from running off the fired ware. Added to these three elements are colour additions. Because each glaze melts at a specific temperature, it is important to check that any glaze that you put on your work is compatible with the temperature of your kiln-firing.

Glaze enhances the colour, texture and design of a piece of work in many ways. Each glaze is made up of different proportions of different materials, often given as recipe ingredients. The ingredients of these recipes dictate the type or characteristic of a glaze and the temperature to which it will fire. Many makers prefer to mix their own glazes from glaze recipes found in books or passed on by word of mouth, while others prefer to use ready-prepared glazes bought from a ceramic supplier.

Raw ceramic materials to make up glazes can be ordered from commercial suppliers. Each material is a dry powder, packaged in a bag, which will not deteriorate with age and can be stored indefinitely in its powder form or as a liquid-glaze mix.

The materials contained in a glaze come from naturally occurring rocks and minerals, such as flint and limestone. The following are some of the more commonly used raw materials for making up a glaze, along with some information on their contribution to a glaze characteristic. This book does not attempt to go into detail about making up or altering your own glaze recipes. As you become more experienced and interested in glaze and the firing process, glaze will become an enticing area of ceramics to explore in greater depth.

Flint and quartz are pure forms of silica rock. They are the main source of glass in a glaze. Adjusting this material in a glaze recipe will increase or reduce crazing.

Alumina makes a glaze more or less fluid, opaque, durable and matt. It can also reduce crawling in a glaze, and can prevent a glaze from crystallising. Most alumina necessary for a glaze is supplied by clay and feldspar.

Ball clay introduces silica and alumina to a glaze. Ball clays vary a great deal, depending on where they are mined. Some are high in silica, others in alumina. Ball clay and china clay are the main ingredients of decorating slips.

China clay, or kaolin, is a suspending agent and introduces silica and alumina to a glaze.

Feldspars are the main fluxes in high-fired glazes and introduce the alkalis sodium and potassium. Each of the 12 feldspars has a different chemical composition, but potash feldspar rather than soda feldspar is used when no specific spar is called for in a recipe.

Nepheline syenite is a middle- to lower-temperature-range flux that introduces higher amounts of the alkalis sodium and potassium and less silica than other feldspars.

Cornish stone (pegmatite) contains a wider combination of fluxes for high-temperature glazes, including sodium, potassium, magnesia and calcium.

Dolomite (calcium magnesium carbonate) introduces magnesium and calcium and gives a glaze an eggshell/vellum-type characteristic.

Whiting (calcium carbonate) gives the colour characteristic of 'celadon' glazes and is craze-resistant. In excess, whiting gives a matt, dull or rough surface to a glaze.

Talc (French talc or soapstone) contains magnesium and gives an opaque, vellum-like finish to a glaze.

Calcium borate frit (colemanite) is used in small quantities in place of colemanite as a flux to intensify glaze colour and reduce crazing. It introduces boron to a glaze.

Pots by Dianne Cross, showing the turquoise colour produced with a barium glaze.

Barium carbonate gives a characteristic, dry glaze of an intense, turquoise-blue colour when combined with copper oxide.

Lithium carbonate or spodumene, which provides good colour response, increases the firing range of a glaze and corrects crazing in a glaze.

Silicon carbide gives a volcanic or pitted quality to a glaze.

Bone ash gives opalescence to a glaze. In high-fired glazes, it is a source of calcium.

Frits

Jane Hanson's bowl decorated with metal oxides.

A frit is a ceramic material that is fused with glass to make any soluble ingredients in a glaze insoluble, and therefore safe to use. Frits introduce fluxes and silica to a glaze. There are three types of lead frit: lead monosilicate, bisilicate and sesquisilicate. Lead is a lower-middle-temperature flux used in oxidised firings only that gives good colour response. Boric oxide in a borax frit reduces crazing and enhances colour, increasing the firing range and durability of a lead glaze. Borax frits vary, so experiments have to be made when a frit quoted in a glaze recipe is not available. Alkaline frits are used in alkaline glazes that contain a high proportion of soda or potash. An alkaline glaze gives copper oxide its characteristic turquoise colour.

Oxides

Glaze oxides should not be confused with metallic oxides for decorating. Some of the more commonly used materials in glaze recipes include magnesium carbonate, which is a high-temperature flux that gives a smooth, fatty surface to a glaze. Zinc oxide is a middle- and high-temperature-range flux used moderately to prevent pinholing. When it is combined with copper oxide, it produces a brilliant turquoise colour. When it is used with titanium, it produces crystalline glazes.

Opacifiers

Opacifiers are materials that make a transparent glaze opaque as an addition of 2–15 per cent. Opacifiers include tin oxide, zirconium oxide (silicate) and titanium oxide. Combined with metallic oxides or stains, they will make an opaque coloured glaze.

US EQUIVALENTS OF **UK** RAW MATERIALS FOR GLAZES

Ball clay: Kentucky OM4, Kentucky Special and Tennessee No. 5.

China clay (kaolin): EPK is a more plastic china clay from Florida.

Feldspar: in the USA, potash is known as Custer Bell, Buckingham G200, Kingham K200, Clinchfield No. 202 and G22; soda is known as F-4 Kona.

Cornish stone: in the USA, this is known as Cornwall, Carolina stone, Kona A-4 and pyrophyllite.

Colemanite: known in the USA as Gerstley Borate. Colemanite is not used in its available European form because it causes the glaze to spit off the surface.

Frits: high-alkaline frits, such as Ferro 3110 and Ferro 5301, have no direct equivalents, and experiments will have to be made to achieve similar effects when translating UK recipes.

Zirconium silicate: in the USA, this is sold under the trade names Opax, Superpax and Zicopax.

Tools

1 Large sieve, support slats (2) and sieving brush (3): used to sieve bucket-sized quantities of glaze. The optimum for sieving ceramic colour is 60–80# (see page 196).

4 Bucket and indelible pen (5): an assortment of plastic ware is necessary for safe, airtight storage. Glazes look very similar when in slop form, so label buckets with an indelible pen and seal them so that they retain water.

6 Mask, surgical gloves (7) and apron (8): precautions should be taken when preparing dry materials to avoid inhaling particles of dust. A mask should meet the appropriate particle-size safety standards (BS60 16 TYPE 2).

9 Glaze mop or soft brush: for touching up missing spots of glaze.

Sponge: for wiping glaze off bases and lid fittings.

10 Wax resist: for excluding glaze from lid-fitting areas.

11 Stiff brushes: for brushing on glazes.

Preparing your glaze

12 Spoon: for mixing glaze.

13 Pouring jug: for pouring glaze.

14 Towel: for drying your hands (glazed work should be handled with dry hands).

When making up a glaze from dry ingredients, place the powder in a sealable bucket at least twice the size of the volume that you are mixing to allow for the addition of approximately 100ml of water to every 100g of powder. Allow the water to soak in thoroughly before going on to the next stage of sieving the ingredients.

Sieving a glaze

To sieve your glaze, pass the wet ingredients through the sieve three times to create a smooth, even mix. If you do not have a sieve brush, then a plastic washing-up brush is fine for the job of pushing the ingredients through the mesh. (For more details on sieving and consistency, see page 173.)

Testing glaze consistency

The correct consistency and thickness of glaze slop will vary according to its type. You can only get to know the correct consistency, or 'cover', of your glaze by firing it to its intended temperature. The general rule is that glaze should be of single-cream consistency, but there are plenty of examples that break this rule. For example, all transparent glazes are applied milk-thin. Mix the glaze thoroughly, then dip a dry finger into it to check its consistency before using it on your work.

When you have sieved your glaze, stir it and check its consistency by dipping a dry finger into it and looking at its coverage. If the mix is too thick, add water a little at a time until it feels right. If it is too thin, you will have to leave it overnight to settle, after which time you can take all of the water off the top by pouring or scooping it away. You can then stir in a little water at a time.

Most glazes settle to the bottom of their containers because of the weight of the particles in suspension. Heavy particles, such as metallic oxides and lead frits, often sink heavily to the bottom of the bucket. If you do not stir your glaze, you will be applying little more than water to your work. A small addition (1–2%) of bentonite in a glaze that is prone to settling will act as a glaze-suspender. Bentonite must be added to the dry materials as it is difficult to mix it into a glaze that is already in slop form.

Snack centre by Angelika Dennis. Glazes can add functionality, as well as beauty.

The most usual reason for a layer of glaze on clay-work is to enable the surface to be cleaned of food when the piece is used for eating and drinking purposes. When applying glaze for this reason, the glaze covering must be applied uniformly.

Another reason for applying glaze might be for decorative purposes, or to enhance colour applied as slips or decoration. Sometimes glaze is applied to one area and not to another to create a contrast between smooth and dry surfaces, or it is pushed into a surface to pick out a textured area using the wash-back technique described in the slip-decorating section (see page 181). In each case, the technique of application will vary according to what you are glazing, how much glaze is available and the character of the glaze.

Lidded, plastic buckets are essential for airtight storage so that glazes do not dry out.

Applying glaze

As a rule, glaze is most often applied to clay at the biscuit stage of the clay cycle. This is to make the process of glazing easier for handling the ware without breakages occurring. There are, however, some makers who single-fire their work, applying all of their decoration and glaze at the leather-hard or bone-dry stage. A high proportion of clay is used to make up single-fire glaze recipes to allow for the shrinkage of the raw clay.

Make sure that your biscuitware is dust- and grease-free when it comes to glazing as dust and grease can stop the glaze from adhering evenly to the clay surface. Work should be glazed swiftly because once the porous, biscuit-fired wall is full of water, it will not pull the glaze evenly onto its surface.

Rule number one when glazing a piece of work is to treat the internal walls first. This is done to prevent any unnecessary handling of the external glaze, which, when unfired, is powdery and easily rubbed off. It also prevents the marring of any carefully applied, unfired designs or decoration.

The technique for glazing internal walls is to pour the glaze into the piece of work using a jug. To do this, first stir the glaze thoroughly and check its consistency. Take enough glaze to fill the vessel as quickly as possible, then, while turning it in both hands, immediately pour out the excess into its appropriate bucket, ensuring that you have covered the entire surface of the inside wall. Any small spots that you miss can be touched up using a soft brush or glaze mop, and any excess spilled onto the outer wall can be wiped back with a damp sponge (but don't oversaturate the bisqued wall).

The reason for performing the task of glazing with speed is to prevent the wall from becoming saturated with the water in the glaze. If the wall does become overly wet, the glaze applied to the outer wall will not adhere to it. The biscuit-fired clay wall will be full, like a wet sponge, and will be unable to soak up the glaze slop. If a piece does become overly saturated, leave it until it has dried and then continue with the glazing.

Unfired glaze sits on the surface of the clay as a layer of powder. It is fragile and needs to be handled with care, so avoid any unnecessary handling or damaging knocks.

Glazing the pinched and coiled bottle

This transparent blue glaze is made by adding 0.5% cobalt oxide to the base alkaline glaze. The bottle is fired slowly to 1,060°C. The glaze has to be of a fairly thick, single-cream consistency to give a good, strong, blue cover to the work.

1. Pour glaze into the inside of an enclosed shape by picking up enough glaze to fill the work approximately half-full, using a jug to tip the glaze in quickly. Pour out the excess while turning the work to cover the entire surface of the internal wall. Wipe back any excess glaze using a damp sponge, being careful not to make the wall too wet. Once the inside has been glazed, the outside covering of glaze can be applied. Stir the glaze well before applying it because glaze settles quickly and you want to achieve a consistent coverage of glaze over your work.

2. To obtain a sufficient depth of glaze to dip the bottle, transfer the glaze to a narrow, plastic bottle. This allows the bottle to be dipped in one go to give an even covering of glaze. To glaze the outside wall of a bottle, grip it at the base and immerse it level with the surface of the glaze. Hold the work in as few places as possible, and preferably at the foot of the piece, to avoid leaving fingermarks on the glaze.

Holding the piece upside down, immerse it quickly under the glaze to the point to which you want the glaze to reach. If the work is held level to the surface of the glaze as it is submerged, a pocket of air will be trapped inside the enclosed shape, preventing a double build-up of glaze on the inside wall. This also makes it possible to use a contrasting-coloured glaze on the external wall of any work that has a level rim that finishes to form a clean line at its edge.

3. When pulling the bottle out of the glaze, tilt it and give it a slight shake to encourage any excess glaze to drip back into the bucket.

Slide the piece, rim facing upwards, onto a board or table edge, being careful not to touch the wet glaze until it is dry. Fill in any missing spots with a soft brush loaded with glaze. Wipe any glaze from the base with a clean, damp sponge before placing the piece in the kiln for the final glaze-firing.

Dipping the beads

A stoneware transparent glaze is used for the beads, and is applied at a thin
consistency, as is usual for a transparent glaze. The glazed beads are then fired to
1,260°C. (See page 241 to see how to place them in the kiln for glaze-firing.)

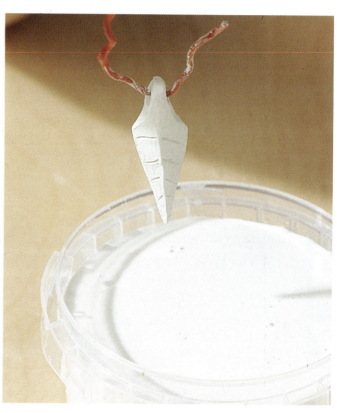

When glaze-dipping any small object, ensure that the glaze is frequently
stirred as glaze that is allowed to settle – even for a short space of time
– will have a skim layer of water that will not give adequate coverage. To
glaze the beads without leaving fingermarks, dip them with the aid of a
piece of wire. The holes of the beads can be freed of glaze by a sharp
blow through the hole before the glaze dries. Alternatively, you could
scrape the glaze out of the holes with the tip of a knife.

Glazing the coiled and carved bird

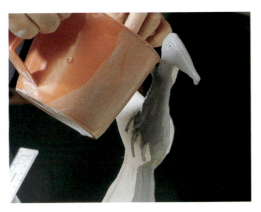

1. If there is insufficient glaze to dip them into it, you can glaze large pieces, such as the bird, by pouring glaze over the work using a jug.

2. The piece is positioned, resting on level slats, over a sufficiently large container.

If a glaze is inappropriate for brushing on, or of an insufficient quantity to enable you to submerge your work in it, it can also be poured over large pieces that are standing either upright or upside down. Rest the work on two slats over a container large enough to catch the poured glaze. Try not to overlap the glaze unless this is the desired effect. Small areas that are missing glaze can be spot-patched rather than making the applied glaze overly thick. Work glazed using this method tends to collect drops of dried glaze at points resting on the slats and requires careful scraping once the glaze is dry to level the glazed surface. If you are turning a piece of work that has a level rim upside down to pour glaze over it, wipe the base free of glaze while it is upside down on the slats to avoid unnecessary handling. This will prevent the powdered glaze at the rim from being damaged when it is dry.

The turquoise glaze used for the bird is a transparent alkaline base with a 3% copper-oxide addition. The bird is fired slowly to 1,060°C.

Brushing glaze onto the hollowed, modelled figure

A brush-on glaze is applied to the carved figure with a stiff brush, pushing the glaze down, into any carved crevices.

A black, brush-on glaze is used for the figure, which is fired to 1,050°C.

Many commercially bought glazes are produced solely for applying with a brush. There are many brush-on glazes in a broad range of colours, fired effects and temperature ranges. Different ceramic suppliers supply their own particular ranges to choose from.

Brush-on glazes have a gelatinous consistency similar to non-drip emulsion paint, and are therefore easier to apply with a stiff brush. For an equivalent covering to poured or dipped glaze, they should be applied using at least two coats, allowing the first to become touch-dry before applying the second.

Brush-on glazes are useful when small quantities of glaze of a particular colour or effect are required. They are easy to use and require no preparation and little of the physical co-ordination needed to pour and dip a glaze. Ensure that the lids of brush-on glazes are fully resealed after each use as they often do not soak back down to slop once they have been allowed to dry out.

It is also possible to apply many slop glazes with a brush, either as an overall covering or as decoration, although some glazes can look patchy and uneven when applied in this way. To discover which glazes are suitable for brushing, look at a fired test result. Wipe back the base of the figure before setting it in the kiln.

Glazing the teapot

The glaze used for the teapot is a white tin glaze that is fired to a temperature of 1,180°C.

1. The inside of the teapot body is glazed first by pouring a jugful of glaze around its inside face and quickly pouring it out. The pouring holes are cleared of glaze by blowing forcibly down the spout before the glaze dries.

2. The inside of the lid is given the same treatment and the outside is then dipped. The job of clearing the glaze from the holes in the lid of the teapot can also be done once the glaze is dry, with a needle or the tip of a knife.

Applying wax resist before glazing

Wax resist is used on the touching areas of the lid and the gallery of the teapot to repel the glaze and ease the task of wiping glaze back before placing it in the kiln to fire. Keeping these two parts free of glaze, the teapot lid can be fired in place in the kiln to give a better lid fit. It is necessary to wipe away any droplets of glaze that have formed on the wax surface using a damp sponge before placing the work in the kiln. Wax resist can only be removed by firing it off in the kiln, so if it happens to drop in the wrong place, it will not be possible to wash it off. Wax-resist solution can also be used on foot-rings or bases to give a clean edge to the applied glaze, and to make the important task of wiping back any glaze less laborious. Allow the wax-resist solution to dry completely in order to act as a repellent.

3. The glaze then is poured over the teapot's outer body.

4. Missing areas are patched with a glaze mop. When the teapot is bone dry, the glaze is pared down to remove any obviously thick areas using a metal-kidney edge or a dry fingertip to even out the powdered glaze.

5. Pinholes or small craters in the powdery-glaze surface can also be rubbed down with a piece of plastic mesh or a dry fingertip once the glaze is completely dry.

6. A little cobalt oxide is mixed with the tin glaze and is then sponge-stamped over the teapot to achieve a polka-dot design.

Glazing the leather-hard-slab box

The inside of the box is glazed first, using a base, matt, transparent glaze that has had 10% black stain added to it. The box is fired slowly to 1,115°C. The stain causes the glaze to become opaque. The same glaze is used on the outside of the box without the stain addition.

1. The black glaze is poured into the box with a jug, is moved around the inside to cover the internal walls, and is then poured out.

2. Glaze is poured over the inside of the lid.

3. Wiping back is done with a damp sponge that is returned to the water to be rinsed as it becomes clogged with the removed glaze.

4. The matt, transparent glaze is applied to the outside of the box with a sponge to ensure an even, thin coverage.

5. The process of wiping back the lid fitting and base of the box is an important part of the finishing work that should be done thoroughly if the piece is not to be left stuck permanently to a kiln shelf, or a lid permanently glued into place. (Lids are fired in place whenever possible.)

Glazing the hump-mould bowl

The glaze used on the bowl is transparent. It is applied thinly and fired to 1,060°C.

1. Before the bowl is glazed, diluted neat cobalt oxide is washed over the textured area of the bowl.

2. A sponge is used to wipe back the cobalt oxide from the raised areas of the textured surface.

3. The bowl is glazed on its upper face first.

4. The slop is poured in with a jug, and the bowl is then tipped in a circular motion to allow the glaze to cover the entire area.

5. The excess glaze is then poured out, over the edge.

6. After the inside face has become touch-dry, the outside of the bowl can be glazed by immersing it, base first, to the rim.

7. Missed spots are spot-patched with a soft brush and the base is wiped free of glaze.

8. The base is wiped free of all glaze with a damp sponge before the work is placed in the kiln for the glaze-firing.

Dipping a bowl with a foot-ring

1. If a bowl has a foot-ring, it can be immersed, rim facing downwards, into the glaze.

2. Immerse the bowl for a count of three.

3. Let any drips fall back into the glaze bucket.

4. Glaze can be poured over the inside of the foot-ring from a jug.

5. The foot-ring need only be wiped back where the bowl will touch the kiln shelf.

Glazing the relief-tile panel

The glaze used on the relief-tile panel is a white tin glaze that is fired to 1,180°C.

1. The glaze is transferred to a wide, shallow tray so that the tile can be dipped in one go to ensure an even surface to the glaze application. The tile is taken through the glaze with a sweeping motion.

2. Once the glaze has become touch-dry, the tile is wiped free of all glaze.

3. Metallic oxides are then brushed or sponged on top of the powdery-glaze surface. The tile is placed on sand on the kiln shelf to help it to move during the firing and so prevent it from cracking.

Glazing the soft-slab dish

The glaze used on the soft-slab dish is a stoneware transparent glaze that was stained with 6% iron oxide. The glaze was then fired to 1,260°C.

1. Sufficient glaze is poured with a jug to cover the inside area of the dish and the rim.

2. The glaze is poured out over the edge. The underside of the rim is also covered at the same time by this method.

The base of the dish is cleaned back thoroughly with a damp sponge before the piece is placed in the kiln for the glaze-firing.

Glazing the jug

The glaze used for the jug is a white tin glaze that is fired to 1,180°C.

1. The inside of the jug is glazed first by tipping in sufficient glaze to …

2. … rotate the glaze to cover the inside area while tipping out the glaze over the rim.

3. The outside of the jug is dipped to a midway point.

Now read the kiln-firing section that follows to find out how to pack and fire glaze-firings.

KILN-FIRING

Once your clay-work is made, it must undergo the heat of the kiln to change the clay both chemically and physically, either to make the clay hard and porous by biscuit-firing, or to melt and fuse the glaze to the clay wall and to make both the glaze and the clay wall hard and permanent. The term for the hardness and fusing of both clay and glaze is 'vitrification'. The amount of vitrification depends on the final temperature and the length of time taken to reach it. The effect of time and heat, known as 'heat-work', varies according to the type of clay and glaze that you are using.

There are many different shapes and sizes of kilns, from bonfire stacks built up from twigs and brushwood and then covered with clay and earth for insulation, through to sophisticated electric or gas kilns that fire to high temperatures and give a highly controlled kiln environment. All kilns, no matter what their size or shape, work on the same principle. The work to be fired is placed in an enclosed chamber through which the heat flows and circulates. The heat in the kiln is directed through, down or up towards a flue or chimney. The control of the heat flow to ensure that the entire kiln fires at an even temperature is called 'draft'. Even in simple electric kilns, consideration of the draft is made when deciding how to space the kiln shelves that support the clay-work in stacks inside the kiln chamber.

Temperature in a kiln is always measured in degrees centigrade (°C). In order to control the firing cycle, the temperature rise and fall of the kiln is paced. Clay needs at least red heat (600°C) to become durable enough to use, and both biscuit- and glaze-

firings require the kiln to pass red heat. A bonfire-type firing
will reach a temperature of around 700°C, while an electric,
gas, solid-fuel or wood-fired kiln is capable of achieving
temperatures of up to 1,300°C. No matter what temperature it
reaches, a kiln-firing takes a number of hours, as the rise to
full temperature and the cooling process are measured
and controlled.

If you want to make or buy your own kiln, deciding factors will
be its volume, the type of work that you want to make, where
the kiln is to be put and the amount of indoor or outdoor space
available. Designing and building a kiln to suit your personal
needs is a practical solution, and there are many instructive
books available on this subject. Specialist tools and materials that
are able to withstand high temperatures, such as refractory bricks
and aluminous cements and mortars, are used to build kilns. If
you are purchasing a ready-made kiln, there are plenty of styles
to choose from. Kilns can be packed from the top or the front,
by lifting in shelves or by sliding shelf stacks into the kiln on a
trolley. Some kilns can be altered in size to suit a particular firing
by adding or taking away clip-on rings made of heat-resistant
material. Some kilns fire on bottled or mains gas and others on
electricity. Your requirements, and the various alternatives
available, need to be considered before you purchase a kiln, even
if you are considering buying second-hand equipment that
you've seen in classified advertisements in specialist magazines.

Equipment

Both top-loading and front-loading electric and gas kilns are built from lightweight refractory bricks, retained in either a steel (in front-loaders) or a stainless-steel (in top-loaders) casing. The lightweight casing on top-loading kilns is efficient insulation and makes them economical to fire, as well as lighter to move and transport.

Two top-loading, electric kilns.

Kilns should be positioned in a situation that allows adequate ventilation to remove the noxious fumes created in the firing. A site removed from the main working or living area is ideal, otherwise it is important to include the extraction of any fumes by means of a chimney hood and fan over the kiln in your installation plans.

There are choices in the equipment available with which to measure, indicate and control the temperature inside the kiln. A pyrometer is used to measure and indicate temperature. It is linked to the temperature-sensor wires inside a porcelain tube, called a thermocouple. This sensor slots through a hole in the kiln wall into the firing chamber. The thermocouple generates a voltage along its wires to the pyrometer, which displays the temperature information. There are two types of pyrometer, analogue and digital. Both pyrometers are accurate, but an analogue pyrometer is easier to read and check. Some pyrometers, called controllers, enable automated control throughout the firing cycle. There are various controllers on the market, ranging from those that provide a cut-off point at the final firing temperature to those that give complete control over the entire firing cycle.

The controller

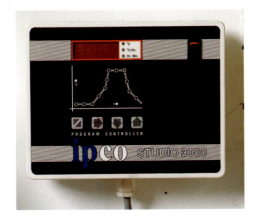

The great advantage of fitting a controller to an electric kiln is that it is possible to leave the kiln unattended while it automatically increases in temperature and then switches off at a pre-set cut-off point. Controllers can be set to control the firing cycle of a kiln, from the time that the firing begins, called 'delay start', through the 'set points' at which the temperature is increased, to the speed of the rise in temperature (called 'ramps'). Additionally, controllers can control the later part of a firing cycle, called 'soaking', which requires the temperature to be held for a measured amount of time. A number of firing programmes can be entered, stored and selected to cover different firings for different firing cycles. Each firing cycle includes necessary set points, ramps and soaks to achieve optimum fired results.

If a controller is not fitted to a top-loading electric kiln, then just the end point of the firing can be controlled with a weighted cut-off switch that is loaded with a temperature bar or cone. This temperature bar is chosen by its number, with each number matching a particular temperature. The minibars used in top-loading electric kilns follow the Orton temperature scale. There are three different temperature-cone scales (as shown on page 235), and it is not unusual for optimum glaze temperatures to be quoted as cone 3, 6 or 8 etc, according to these scales.

The kiln-sitter that houses the temperature cone on a top-loading electric kiln gives a reliable temperature reading because it melts and bends according to heat work. The term 'heat work' indicates that it is not just the final temperature of a kiln-firing that is important, but also the amount of time that is taken to achieve that temperature.

Pyrometric cones and minibars

1 Pyrometric minibars for a cut-off firing controller.
2 Standard pyrometric cones.

Pyrometric cones and minibars give an accurate indication of 'heat work' inside the kiln. Temperature cones are numbered according to the temperature at which they melt and bend. A number of different ranges of cones exist, including Orton, Seger and Harrison, in varying temperatures and corresponding numbers that can be intermixed within a set of cones.

Standard pyrometric cones bend at set temperatures according to their number. They are placed in the kiln chamber in view of the spyhole. As each cone bends, it indicates that the temperature of that cone has been reached. The lowest-temperature cone is set at the front of the line of cones.

Conversion chart for temperature, Staffordshire cones, Seger cones and Orton cones*

°C & colour in the kiln	°F	Staffordshire cones	Seger cones	Orton cones
635 *dull red-orange*	1,175	020	–	–
710	1,310	018	018	–
720	1,328	–	–	018
770	1,418	–	–	017
Onglaze 760–840°C				
790	1,454	015	015a	–
815	1,499	014	014a	–
830	1,526	–	014	–
855 *red-orange*	1,571	012	–	–
860	1,580	–	012a	013
900	1,652	010	011a	–
905	1,661	–	–	011
940	1,724	08	09a	–
950	1,742	08	09a	–
970 *orange*	1,778	–	07a	07
980	1,796	06	06a	–
Biscuit 980–1,000°C				
1,000	1,832	05	05a	–
1,015	1,859	–	–	06
Earthenware 950–1,160°C				
1,020	1,868	04	04a	–
1,040	1,904	03	–	05
1,060	1,940	02	03a	04
1,080	1,976	01	02a	–
1,100	2,012	1	01a	–
1,115	2,039	–	–	03
1,120	2,048	2	–	–
1,125	2,057	–	1a	02
1,140	2,084	3	–	–
1,150	2,102	–	2a	01
1,162	2,124	–	–	2
Stoneware 1,200–1,300°C				
Wear eye protection				
1,200 *bright orange*		2,192	6	4a
1,205	2,201	–	–	6
1,230	2,246	7	–	7
Bone china 1,240–1,260°C				
1,250	2,282	8	–	8
Porcelain 1,280–1,300°C				
1,260 *bright yellow*	2,300	8a	7	9
1,280	2,336	9	8	–
1,285	2,345	–	–	10
1,300	2,372	10	9	–
1,305	2,381	–	–	11
1,320	2,408	11	10	–
1,325	2,417	–	–	12
1,335	2,435	–	11	13

*This chart is for large cones only.

Packing the kiln for a biscuit-firing

The first firing, known as the biscuit-firing, takes place when the work is absolutely dry. You can identify this bone-dry stage when the clay has become lighter in colour over its entire surface. At this stage of bone-dryness, the work is very fragile, brittle and easily broken. It is therefore vital to handle the work carefully as you place it in the kiln for biscuit-firing. Do not, for example, pick up your work by the rim, but lift it with both hands around the base.

Check that work is bone dry before packing a biscuit-fire kiln. In a biscuit-firing, clay-work can touch and small pieces can be stacked inside larger pieces.

The way in which the kiln is packed for biscuit-firing is very different to that for a glaze-firing. For a biscuit-firing, clay-work can touch: work can be stacked rim to rim and small pieces can be placed inside larger ones. Lids are fired in place (as in glaze-firings). Work can be placed in stacks that are stable and not so heavy that the top weight might crack the supporting work underneath. If the stack is too tall, or the weight of a piece is too great, then another kiln shelf is necessary to take the weight of the pack off the underlying work.

The kiln shelves are set in place in the kiln resting on three columns of kiln props. The separating kiln props are positioned with two props at each corner of one end of the shelf and one at the centre of the other end of the shelf. The kiln props are set at equal heights appropriate to the height of the work that is to be placed in the kiln. To get as much work into the kiln-firing as possible without wasting space, choose work of similar heights to sit on each shelf, or choose to pack work that can stack to equal heights. This makes the kiln as economical as possible to fire. Pack any small work to the centre or the top of the kiln and ensure that the first shelf of the stack is packed with the tallest work. Working on the theory that heat rises, this will allow the heat to circulate freely in the firing chamber.

Large, flat pieces that might break if anything is stacked on top of them can be placed on sand to allow equal movement of the work during shrinkage and to prevent it from cracking.

Sand is placed under objects that cover a broad area, such as tiles or large, thick, sculptural pieces.

Packing the kiln for a glaze-firing

Any area of glaze that touches a kiln shelf must be completely wiped away with a damp sponge before packing work into a kiln for a glaze-firing.

Any glaze that has been applied to the exterior of a piece of work must be cleared away from points that will touch a kiln shelf when the work is placed in the kiln. Before placing any work to be fired in the kiln, it is vital to check that the bases are free of glaze. Bases and foot-rings must be wiped clean of any glaze with a damp sponge before work is packed into the kiln to be fired, unless it is to be set on a stilt. Lid fittings must also be wiped free of all glaze so that, wherever possible, lids can be fired in place to ensure a good fit.

Glaze can remain on a base if a low-fired piece is to be set for firing on a stilt (see page 240). Razor-sharp stilt scars are removed using a Carborundum stone once the work has been fired. Glazing the base of an earthenware piece will impair the 'weeping' of any water that occurs if a clay body is not fully vitrified. Stilt-firing is inappropriate for high-fired work, which will not 'weep', and quite often warps if set for firing on a stilt.

If you have new kiln furniture, your shelves should be given a coat of bat wash bought ready-made to be mixed with water or made up from two parts alumina hydrate and one part china clay. Mixed into a milk consistency, bat wash is painted onto kiln shelves to prevent glazed work from sticking to them. (Putting bat wash on your kiln shelves does *not* mean that you do not have to wipe back glaze from points of contact with the kiln shelf!)

Once your biscuit-fired work is glazed, it must be handled with great care when packing it into the kiln to avoid damaging the surface of the applied glaze. Once the glaze is dry, it is easy to rub or knock the powdery particles off, particularly on sharp edges, such as rims.

Stack your kiln shelves in the same way as for a biscuit-firing, arranging the work for each shelf into equal, or near-equal, heights. The separating kiln props are positioned in groups of three, with two props at each corner of one end of the shelf and one at the centre of the other end of the shelf. This will prevent the kiln shelves from warping at high temperatures and will provide maximum stability to the packed stack of shelves and work. Pack any small work to the centre or the top of the kiln, and ensure that the first (or bottom) shelf of the stack is packed with the tallest work. This will allow the heat to circulate freely in the firing chamber.

Unlike for the biscuit-firing, each piece must sit separately on the shelf, without touching the piece next to it. Each piece of your work must therefore be placed on the kiln shelf separately. (If your work is to be low-fired and you prefer the base to be glazed, the work can be placed on a stilt.) As well as checking the bases of your work, ensure that your lid fittings are free from glaze on both contacting surfaces so that you can fire the lids in place.

Kiln furniture

Kiln furniture used for separating shelves in the firing chamber to make economical use of space.

I A castellated shelf prop.
2 A firing stilt. The sharp scar left on a piece by a stilt after glaze-firing is removed by rubbing it down with a Carborundum stone.
3 A flat-topped shelf prop.

Kiln furniture is made from a high-firing, refractory material that can withstand high temperatures without warping. The furniture is used for separating work in the kiln-firing, while also making full and economic use of the space in the firing chamber. Kiln shelves are stacked alternately on three piers of kiln props that are set directly above one another at each layer. Kiln shelves should not fit exactly to the edges of the inside of the kiln, but must be 2–5cm away from the kiln sides, depending on the size of the firing chamber. The heat can then circulate freely around the firing chamber. Stilts are used to support work with glazed bases to prevent contact with the kiln shelves; tiles and plate racks (not shown in the above picture) allow flatware items to be packed while making economic use of kiln space.

BEAD RACK

The problem of how to fire glazed beads that cannot be placed on the kiln shelf if the entire surface of the bead is to be fired is solved with the use of Nichrome wire, which will not melt in the kiln. Bead racks suspend each bead off the kiln shelf. They can be bought ready-made from ceramic suppliers or else can be made with clay and Nichrome wire to custom-fit your beads.

BISCUIT-FIRING

Biscuit-firing clay-work to around 980–1,100°C makes the ware porous and gives physical strength for further decoration and glazing. Firing any higher than these temperatures would make the clay dense and vitrified, and therefore difficult to glaze for the next firing stage. Some clay-makers prefer to leave out the biscuit-firing stage altogether and instead single-fire their work. This is possible if you have a suitable glaze to apply to the clay before it is biscuit-fired. The type of glaze suitable for single-fire purposes has a high clay content, and will therefore shrink at the same rate as the clay when drying and firing, without peeling or falling away from the clay wall.

Whether you are single-firing or biscuit-firing, the firing cycle is exactly the same. What you are doing in such firings is taking bone-dry clay and heating it in the kiln. The initial stage of this firing is a very slow build-up in temperature to remove any water in the clay. It is important to take particular care with large, thick pieces of clay-work, leaving them for many days in a warm environment to dry thoroughly before they are placed in the kiln. The drying process is completed at 100°C in the initial stages of the biscuit-firing. This point is known as water-smoking, when the water leaves the clay as steam. It is at this early point in the firing that work can explode in the kiln if it is too wet and heated too fast. It is the escaping steam that literally pushes the clay wall apart, and not expanding air pockets in the clay, as is commonly believed. Chemically combined water is further removed from the clay at 350°C, and during both of these water-smoking stages, any vents in the kiln should remain open to allow the water vapour to exit the kiln.

It is very important to raise the temperature extremely slowly during this early stage of firing, particularly with pieces with thick wall sections (over 0.5cm thick). The rate of climb in temperature should be around 50ºC per hour, until the kiln has reached red heat. 'Quartz inversion' is the term that describes the chemical change that takes place when the crystals contained in the clay body increase in size and rearrange themselves. This occurs at 227ºC and at 577ºC, and is another crucial point in the firing process that should proceed slowly in order to prevent the work from cracking due to rapid heating or cooling. The hairline-type cracks that occur for this reason are known by the firing-fault term 'dunting'.

The quartz inversion is repeated in reverse at the cooling stage of the kiln-firing, which should not be hurried by opening vents or doors. Because of these quartz-inversion points in the firing cycle, it is safe to assume that when the firing has reached 600°C, or red heat, it is safe to turn up the rate of incline or the ramp and to close any vents. When the kiln is cooling, it is best to assume that the kiln door cannot be safely opened until the kiln has cooled below 200°C, to around 100–150°C. At approximately 600°C, sintered strength occurs when all of the water is driven out. At this point, the particles in the clay and glaze have rearranged themselves, becoming solid by sticking to one another, yet without having fused.

Ivar Mackay's copper-red-on-white pedestal bowl. This piece was biscuit-fired before glazing.

Biscuit- and single-firing

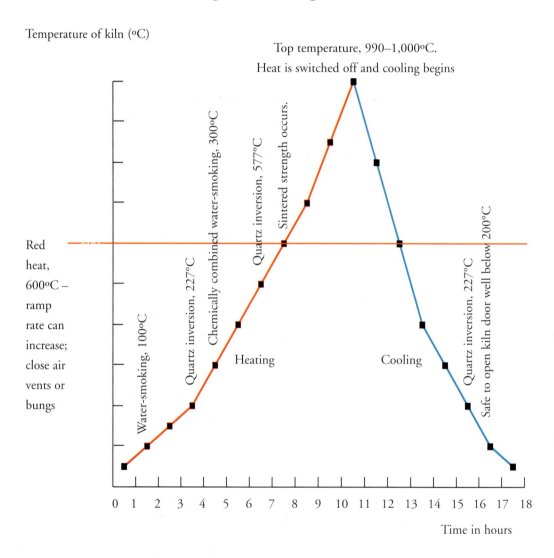

Temperature of kiln (°C)

Top temperature, 990–1,000°C.

Heat is switched off and cooling begins

Red heat, 600°C – ramp rate can increase; close air vents or bungs

Sintered strength occurs.

Quartz inversion, 577°C

Chemically combined water-smoking, 300°C

Quartz inversion, 227°C

Water-smoking, 100°C

Heating

Cooling

Quartz inversion, 227°C

Safe to open kiln door well below 200°C

Time in hours

Temperature rises will vary according to the size of the kiln and the density of the kiln pack. This firing chart therefore provides only a rough guide to firing times.

GLAZE-FIRING

Described as the 'set point' on a temperature controller, the final temperature is decided by which glaze you have chosen to apply to your fired work. The maturing temperature point of that particular glaze gives your final temperature. As with a biscuit-firing, a glaze-firing should start slowly to drive out any moisture taken into the biscuitware from glazing. After an initial two-hour period, the rate of climb can be increased and vents closed.

When the clay-work is subjected to heat in the kiln, the clay slips and the glaze melt and fuse, particularly during high-temperature firings (stoneware temperatures). This fusion of the materials is called interface, and it is this melting bond that secures the glaze to the clay. At the lower end of the temperature range (earthenware temperatures), there is less interface or fusion of the glaze and clay, which explains why the colours and decoration often appear to sit under the glaze with little interreaction.

Earthenware-glaze temperatures range from 950°C to 1,150°C. Stoneware- and porcelain-glaze temperatures range from 1,200°C to 1,300°C.

As well as measuring heat-work by placing pyrometric cones in the kiln, heat in the kiln can be gauged visually by the colour in the firing chamber. At 1,100°C, the colour is orangey-red; at 1,200°C, the orange brightens; and at 1,260°C, there is a change to bright yellow. (Do not stare into the kiln for long periods of time, and protect your eyes from the glare of heat by wearing infrared-light-using goggles if you want to test this theory.) As the temperature rises in the kiln, vitrification takes place, and as the final glaze temperature nears, the glaze bubbles and craters form as gas escapes through the glaze layer. This bubbling of the glaze surface is more evident in some glazes than others, and can cause such defects as bloating (bubbles of solidified glaze) or pinholing (small crater holes in the surface of the glaze). By maintaining the kiln temperature at a constant temperature for a number of hours at the end point of the firing (this is called 'soaking'), these defects can be eliminated by allowing the molten glaze time to settle again to a smooth surface once the gas omissions have occurred. The kiln can then be turned off and left to cool.

John Pollex's small jug.

Reduction-firing

All kilns are capable of providing an oxidising atmosphere in the firing chamber. This describes the unrestricted flow and circulation of air passing through the kiln. The second type of atmosphere in a kiln is called 'reduction', and this can only be achieved in kilns that are fired by a live-flame fuel, such as wood, oil or gas. Creating a reduction atmosphere in a kiln involves restricting the passage of secondary air into the kiln, and in so doing starving the kiln atmosphere of oxygen. Reduction-firing can be used for high-temperature or stoneware glazes. This type of firing transforms the glaze by taking up the chemically combined oxygen in the metal oxides of the clay and glaze. The oxygen is required to keep the oxygen-starved atmosphere of the kiln alive. A characteristic glaze result from such a firing includes copper turning blood red in 'sang-boeuf' glazes.

Mandy Parslow's 'tipsy bowls', which were fired in a reducing atmosphere in the kiln.

Glaze-firing

This chart shows temperature-rise rates for reduction and oxidised firing for earthenware-, stoneware- and porcelain-temperature glaze-firings.

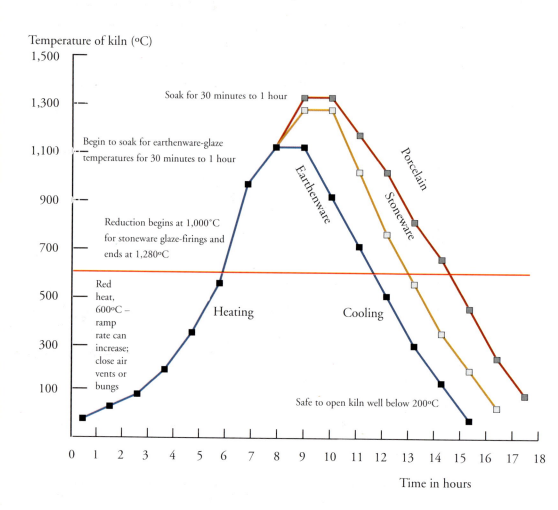

Temperature of kiln (ºC)

Soak for 30 minutes to 1 hour

Begin to soak for earthenware-glaze temperatures for 30 minutes to 1 hour

Reduction begins at 1,000˚C for stoneware glaze-firings and ends at 1,280ºC

Red heat, 600ºC – ramp rate can increase; close air vents or bungs

Heating

Cooling

Earthenware

Stoneware

Porcelain

Safe to open kiln well below 200ºC

Time in hours

ENAMEL-FIRING
(CHINA-PAINTING OR ONGLAZE)

Enamel-firings are relatively fast compared to other types of firing as the approximate final temperature is around 750°C. The temperatures at which onglazes fuse with the glaze vary according to the colours used. The firing involves fusing the colour into the softened glaze, often using successive firings to create overlapping, mixed hues and depth of colour. At the initial stages of the firing, the kiln vent is left open to allow the evaporating painting mediums to escape the kiln as they burn away.

Temperature of kiln (ºC)

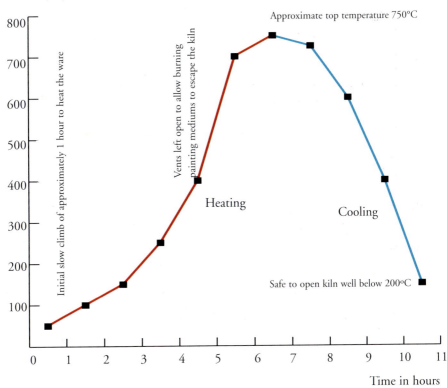

Approximate top temperature 750°C

Vents left open to allow burning painting mediums to escape the kiln

Initial slow climb of approximately 1 hour to heat the ware

Heating

Cooling

Safe to open kiln well below 200ºC

Time in hours

GLOSSARY

Alkaline glaze A glaze in which the main fluxes are alkalies, such as sodium or potassium.

Ball clay Plastic, fine-grained clay used to increase plasticity in clay bodies and to put silica and alumina into glazes.

Banding wheel A turntable on which to make or decorate clay-work, heavy versions of which are used for banding-on lines of colour.

Base set The board on which a model sits that is used to support the cottle wall when mould-making.

Bas relief Three-dimensional modelling raised above a flat surface of clay.

Blistering Bubbles and craters caused by gases escaping from a glaze.

Celadon glaze A grey-green glaze of Chinese origin, the colour being made from iron oxide.

Colour An overall term to include oxides, underglaze colours and stains.

Cottle (USA: coddle) A retaining wall into which plaster is poured for making working plaster moulds or models.

Crawling A glaze defect characterised by the glaze parting and rolling back to leave a bare patch.

Crazing A glaze defect characterised by a network of fine cracks.

Dunting A firing fault characterised by fine, hairline cracks.

Engobe A decorating slip that is halfway between a glaze because it contains a proportion of flux.

Facing up The application of a separating agent, such as soft soap, to a plaster face.

Foot The base of a piece of clay-work.

Gallery The shelf on a pot rim and the extended collar of a lid that secures the lid in its position and prevents it from tipping out when tilted.

Grog Ground, fired clay in various particle sizes that provides workable strength by opening a clay body and enables it to dry uniformly without warping.

Heat-work The combination of temperature and time during a kiln-firing.

Lead glaze A low-temperature glaze in which the main flux is lead.

Leather-hard The stage reached by clay after drying from the plastic state whereby it is firm enough to pick up without distorting, but workable to cut, pare, turn or fettle, join clay additions, apply with slip (or glaze for single-firing) and burnish.

Medium A liquid in which a pigment, such as as an oxide or enamel, is suspended.

Overfire	When a glaze or clay body has exceeded its firing-range temperature.
Oxidation	The firing atmosphere in a kiln that contains enough oxygen to allow the metals in clays, glazes and colours to produce their oxide colours. Electric kilns always produce oxidising firings.
Oxide	A combination of an element with oxygen. Most ceramic raw materials consist of oxides. Basic oxides are metals, and acid oxides are non-metals.
Pinholing	A glaze defect caused by bubbles forming in the glaze-firing, which have not had sufficient time to heal over.
Plasticity	The workability of clay that can be sensed when in use.
Porosity	The capacity of plaster or biscuit-fired clay to take up water.
Pyrometer	An instrument for gauging and displaying temperature that is linked to a thermocouple in the kiln's firing chamber.
Pyrometric cones	Cones made from compressed, ceramic materials designed to give a graduated scale of fusing temperatures at approximately 20°C intervals.
Quartz inversion	The point of firing at which crystals of quartz in the clay body physically change, increasing in particle size, and that revert when the kiln is cooled.
Refractory	A term used to describe a material that is able to withstand high temperatures.
Rib	A smooth, shaped tool used to apply even pressure when throwing.
Roulette	A wheel used to imprint a circuit of design onto clay.
Sang boeuf	(or sang-de-boeuf)a deep-red-purplish glaze coloured by copper oxide in a reduction-firing.
Slaking	Soaking down bone-dry clay by covering it in water.
Slip	A homogenous liquid clay that can be coloured with the addition of stains or oxides and used for decorating.
Slip-trailer	A tool used to trail lines or dots of liquid decorating medium onto a clay surface.
Slop	A wet, sieved material ready for use or application.
Slurry	A mixture of clay and water.
Soaking	The point in a firing cycle at which the temperature of a kiln is held for a set length of time.
Sprig	Relief ornament applied to the clay surface at the leather-hard stage, which is produced by pressing clay into a plaster (or clay) sprig mould.
Stilt	A three-pointed, refractory support, used to raise glazed clay-work off its base when in place for firing.
Test piece	A tile or pot that is used to test-fire colours or glazes.
Thermal shock	Extreme, sudden changes of temperature that can cause ceramic ware to crack.

Thixotropic	The property of a slip to change fluidity when left undisturbed.
Underglaze	Decorated colour applied under a glaze that is transparent. The term can also apply to any colour decoration using oxides, commercial underglazes or commercial glaze and body stains.
Underfired	When a glaze or clay body has not reached its optimum firing temperature.
Viscosity	A term applied to glaze when describing its movement when fired. A glaze when fired and fluid has a low viscosity; a glaze when fired and matt or dry has a high viscosity.
Vitrified	The point at which materials in the clay body become fluxed to a dense, hard, non-porous state.
Warping	Movement in a formed shape that occurs when drying or firing.

BIBLIOGRAPHY

Birks, Tony, *The Complete Potter's Companion,* Conran.

Blandino, B, *Coiled Pottery,* A & C Black.

Byers, Ian, *Raku,* Batsford.

Carnegy, D, *Tin-glazed Earthenware,* A & C Black.

Ceramic Review: The International Magazine of Ceramic Art & Craft (www.ceramicreview.com).

Constant, C, & Ogden, S, *The Potter's Palette,* Apple.

Cooper, Emmanuel, *Glazes,* Batsford.

Firth, Donald, *Mold-making for Ceramics,* Krause.

Giorgini, S, *Handmade Tiles,* David & Charles.

Levy, Mike, *Decorated Earthenware,* Batsford.

Phethean, Richard, & Warshaw, Josie, *Throwing Pottery Masterclass,* Anness Publishing.

Phillips, Anthony, *Slips & Slipware,* Batsford.

Rhodes, D, *Clay & Glazes for the Potter,* A & C Black.

Walter, Jane, *Handbuilt Ceramics,* Batsford.

Wondraush, M, *Slipware,* A & C Black.

Wren, Rosemary, *Animal Forms,* Batsford.

INDEX

CREDITS AND ACKNOWLEDGEMENTS

Thanks to all of my clay mentors.
Thanks also to Paul for the use of his
studio for photos, and to Steve
Rafferty at Ceramatech for his prompt
delivery and great service.